P9-CKX-776

The New Politics of Masculinity

The field of masculinities research continues to expand, and has become increasingly complex. Much of the contemporary analysis of men, masculinity and power has been influenced by the work of a number of profeminist writers who have been leading figures in developing new political interventions around men's identities and power. These men have been at the forefront of interrogations of the concept of masculinity and have attempted to develop new forms of radical gender-conscious politics for men who seek to extend gender justice.

The New Politics of Masculinity is the first single-authored feminist text to engage critically with the theoretical frameworks which leading profeminist writers have developed in the field of masculinity studies. Drawing on new social movement and contemporary theory, the book examines the different models of politics that such writers have evolved for men who want to challenge dominant forms of masculinities and inequitable gender relationships. It also assesses the broader effects – on the field of men and masculinities research – of these writers' diverse theorisations of key political concepts such as masculinity, subjectivity, power and resistance.

Overall, *The New Politics of Masculinity* outlines the central theoretical issues for scholars and students working in the area of critical studies of masculinities, and evaluates the effects of men's gender-conscious politics on feminist scholarship and research. *The New Politics of Masculinity* will be of great interest to students and scholars of gender theory, sociology, and politics.

Fidelma Ashe is Lecturer in Politics at the University of Ulster. She is co-author of *Contemporary Social and Political Theory: An Introduction*.

Routledge Innovations in Political Theory

1 **A Radical Green Political Theory**
Alan Carter

2 **Rational Woman**
A feminist critique of dualism
Raia Prokhovnik

3 **Rethinking State Theory**
Mark J. Smith

4 **Gramsci and Contemporary Politics**
Beyond pessimism of the intellect
Anne Showstack Sassoon

5 **Post-Ecologist Politics**
Social theory and the abdication of the ecologist paradigm
Ingolfur Blühdorn

6 **Ecological Relations**
Susan Board

7 **The Political Theory of Global Citizenship**
April Carter

8 **Democracy and National Pluralism**
Edited by Ferran Requejo

9 **Civil Society and Democratic Theory**
Alternative voices
Gideon Baker

10 **Ethics and Politics in Contemporary Theory**
Between critical theory and post-marxism
Mark Devenney

11 **Citizenship and Identity**
Towards a new republic
John Schwarzmantel

12 **Multiculturalism, Identity and Rights**
Edited by Bruce Haddock and Peter Sutch

13 **Political Theory of Global Justice**
A cosmopolitan case for the world state
Luis Cabrera

14 **Democracy, Nationalism and Multiculturalism**
Edited by Ramón Maiz and Ferrán Requejo

15 **Political Reconciliation**
Andrew Schaap

16 **National Cultural Autonomy and Its Contemporary Critics**
Edited by Ephraim Nimni

17 **Power and Politics in Post structuralist Thought**
New theories of the political
Saul Newman

18 **Capabilities Equality**
Edited by Alexander Kaufman

19 **Morality and Nationalism**
Catherine Frost

20 **Principles and Political Order**
The challenge of diversity
Edited by Bruce Haddock, Peri Roberts and Peter Sutch

21 **European Integration and the Nationalities Question**
Edited by John McGarry and Michael Keating

22 **Deliberation, Social Choice and Absolutist Democracy**
David van Mill

23 **Sexual Justice / Cultural Justice**
Critical perspectives in political theory and practice
Edited by Barbara Arneil, Monique Deveaux, Rita Dhamoon and Avigail Eisenberg

24 **The International Political Thought of Carl Schmitt**
Terror, liberal war and the crisis of global order
Edited by Louiza Odysseos and Fabio Petito

25 **In Defense of Human Rights**
A non-religious grounding in a pluralistic world
Ari Kohen

26 **Logics of Critical Explanation in Social and Political Theory**
Jason Glynos and David Howarth

27 **Political Constructivism**
Peri Roberts

28 **The New Politics of Masculinity**
Men, power and resistance
Fidelma Ashe

The New Politics of Masculinity

Men, power and resistance

Fidelma Ashe

LONDON AND NEW YORK

First published 2007
by Routledge
2 Park Square, Milton Park, Abingdon, Oxon OX14 4RN

Simultaneously published in the USA and Canada
by Routledge
270 Madison Avenue, New York, NY 10016

Routledge is an imprint of the Taylor & Francis Group, an informa business

Typeset in Sabon by
Taylor & Francis Books
Printed and bound in Great Britain by
TJ International Ltd, Padstow, Cornwall

British Library Cataloguing in Publication Data
A catalogue record for this book is available from the British Library

Library of Congress Cataloging in Publication Data
Ashe, Fidelma, 1965-
The new politics of masculinity : men, power, and resistance / Fidelma Ashe.

cm. – (Routledge innovations in political theory ; 28)

ISBN 978-0-415-30275-3 (cloth : alk. paper) – ISBN 978-0-203-50836-7 (ebook : alk. paper) 1. Men–Social conditions. 2. Male feminists. 3. Men–Identity. 4. Masculinity. 5. Feminism. I. Title.

2007018417

ISBN13: 978-0-415-30275-3 (hbk)
ISBN13: 978-0-203-50836-7 (ebk)

For Cahal and Lorna

Contents

Acknowledgements

I am indebted to a number of people for their support, insight and encouragement during the development and writing of this book. Chapters 5 and 7 of the book draw on some ideas I tentatively explored during the completion of my PhD thesis at Queen's University in Belfast. I would like thank Shane O'Neill for supervising that thesis, Moya Lloyd for her comments on it and Ian McKenzie for acting as internal examiner. Chapter 5 borrows from an article published in the *Journal of Men and Masculinities* in 2004. I am grateful to the editor of this journal for kind permission to reproduce aspects of the arguments in this article.

During the writing of the book I benefited greatly from the support of colleagues in the School of Economics and Politics at the University of Ulster. Grateful thanks to the politics team. Hazel Henderson provided much needed secretarial support and the Social and Policy Research Institute provided much needed financial support. My head of school, Carmel Roulston, generously read and commented on the majority of the manuscript. Heartfelt thanks goes to Carmel for her support, advice and especially for her willingness to provide practical support when it was so badly needed during the last months of completing the manuscript.

As always I have to thank my friends and family who have in different ways helped me complete this manuscript. My son Cahal and my father William listened patiently to the trials and tribulations of writing the book. Gillian McClelland generously helped with proofreading. Lorna Trainor and her partner have quite simply been amazing friends. I would also like to thank Elisabeth Bethal and Seana McCoy for their friendship, humour and kind support during the writing of the book.

Lastly I would like to give special thanks to Jeff Hearn and Terrell Carver. Jeff very kindly read and commented on the entire manuscript.

His expertise, advice and generosity were invaluable and helped strengthen many aspects of the book. Needless to say I am indebted to Jeff for all his help and interest in the project. Terrell acted as external examiner on my PhD thesis, and without his words of encouragement it is likely that this book would not have been written.

1 Introduction

Issues surrounding men and masculinities have become 'hot politics' in late capitalist societies. Much of the new focus on men's identities has been a consequence of structural changes in contemporary societies interacting with the social and political effects of feminism. The new politics of masculinity is rooted in the claim that the social, political and economic conditions of late capitalist societies have exerted pressure on men's traditional roles and identities, producing a generation of men less secure than their fathers were about their place and function in society.

The restructuring of the family, a changing workplace, the expansion of equality legislation, the challenges of feminism and alternative sexualities have all opened social debate around men's subjectivities and 'proper' social roles. The political discussions that have surrounded men's identities have meant that men, the traditional 'genderless masters' of public/political arenas, have been publicly and politically interrogated as gendered subjects; and more specifically as problematic gendered subjects. Men's gender identities are now a political matter: a cause of concern.

The key terms that have emerged in popular discourses about the plight of the modern man have been 'crisis', 'loss' and 'change'. The 'crisis of masculinity' thesis implies that the old certainties surrounding men's traditional roles in the family and workplace have been swept away through social changes and increases in women's equality, leaving the modern man dazed and confused about his roles and place in society. The qualities of 'manliness' have also been framed as under threat, attacked and undermined by feminism, gay culture and commercialism. The idea that men's losses have resulted in equality gains for women has been common in recent discussions about 'male' crisis. Such claims have at times created the illusion that women are winning the 'sex war'.

Feminists have continually tried to pour cold water over assertions that there has been a significant transfer of power from men to women. Regardless of feminist attempts to develop a more measured assessment of social changes, sections of the Western media have continued to peddle claims that masculinity is in crisis. The popular press has increasingly portrayed modern man as a beleaguered figure suffering under the twin pressures of post-modern culture and post-feminist society.

In a changing social environment of working women, smaller families and high divorce rates, media discussions of gender relationships in the early 1990s led to the appearance of a more narcissistic and child-centred 'new man': a paragon of post-feminist masculinity. Susan Moore (1998) quipped at the time that one of the problems with this man was that he could not be found outside of his media representations.

However, the new politics of masculinity has implications far beyond the media's exaggerated claims about a new generation of 'nappy happy' fathers. Changes in men's identities are rooted in concrete social changes such as globalisation and economic restructuring. Moreover, increased social focus on men as a gendered category has also opened a discursive space around men's identities, roles and power. For example, governments, non-governmental organisations and transnational institutions have integrated concerns about men's changing social roles and identities into their agendas, and have engaged in discussing issues about men within this new interrogative space.

These are just a few examples to illustrate the new concentration on men in the contemporary period. More broadly a range of diverse and often conflicting discourses about men marks current social discussions about gender relationships and identities. Public discourses about men therefore have a degree of fluidity, and emerge in different institutional, political, organisational and geographical contexts. Many of these shifting discourses about men and masculinity are found in more concentrated forms in organisations and networks that instantiate men's identities as a foundation for politics: in other words, forms of politics associated with men's groups. Such groups have developed more structured agendas around issues relating to men in contemporary societies.

Men's gender politics

Men's groups started to emerge in the 1960s and represent a new form of political activism by men around their gendered identities.

These new models of political practice by men have appeared in profeminist and anti-feminist forms. Anti-feminist groups are generally orientated towards stalling or overturning the effects of feminism on contemporary cultures. In contrast, profeminist groups align with feminist perspectives and challenge the standpoints and agendas of non-feminist groups. Profeminist men's politics is therefore orientated towards developing oppositional strategies to provoke changes in gendered power relationships and men's traditional identities. This means that these men have tried to forge an oppositional form of gender politics within cultural contexts that have developed ongoing dialogues around the position of men.

Challenging men's subjectivities and power have been important dimensions of contemporary feminism. Profeminists have been at the forefront of thinking through the possibilities of reinventing men's identities and gender relationships beyond traditional models. Profeminist writers and activists have also had a significant impact on the academic field of gender studies, developing methodologies and theoretical frameworks for studying men and masculinities. Moreover, as this volume illustrates, profeminist standpoints have intermittently and unevenly influenced mainstream politics.

This book considers the perspectives and political practices that have emerged within profeminism. It discusses how this dimension of men's gender politics has engaged with the broader social discourses that have surrounded masculinity in contemporary culture, and it assesses the standpoints and practices that profeminism has developed for men interested in changing men and society in feminist directions. This analysis of profeminism is also orientated towards charting the effects of profeminist practices on the field of oppositional gendered politics more generally. Overall it investigates the theoretical tools and forms of political engagement that profeminism offers to oppositional gendered politics in a context increasingly concerned with masculinity.

Feminists have already engaged with profeminist politics. This book adopts a slightly different approach to the existing feminist literature on men's gender-conscious politics. Feminist commentators on profeminist politics have generally tended to treat profeminism as a homogenous group or movement. This volume attempts to illustrate how different strands of profeminism have framed and developed different forms of politics which engender different political effects. Paying attention to the various and often conflictual models of politics that have emerged in profeminism exposes the dynamics of this form of gendered politics and illustrates the internal struggles that have emerged in profeminism around issues of theory and political practice. However, like other feminist studies of profeminism, this book continues to suggest that oppositional gender politics needs to be wary of some formulations of profeminist standpoints and agendas for change.

Framework

Profeminism is made up of a network of small groups struggling around issues relating to men's power and identities. These groups share similar concerns and try to generate progressive change in the arena of gender relationships. While bound together through this common concern, different profeminist groups have developed divergent ways of 'doing' profeminism. Groups involved in profeminist politics often have their own unique features and can exhibit different mixes of standpoints and practices. These groups' diverse practices and standpoints have generated a range of concerns about the effects of profeminist theory and practice. These concerns have led to debates within profeminism and have generated discussions between feminists and profeminists about the direction of profeminism and its political effects.

The areas of contention that have emerged from these discussions have been considered most consistently and systematically by a number of prominent profeminist writers. Therefore the complexities, strategies and possible power-effects of profeminist politics have been articulated and discussed in more condensed ways by these writers. The different profeminist standpoints that each of the writers examined in this book have developed means that each has articulated different models of profeminist politics. These standpoints and models feed into and often inform debate and perspectives at the more diverse, fluid and less structured level of profeminist activity. This volume concentrates on the work of specific commentators on men and masculinity and profeminist politics to gain access to debates within and around profeminism. While the book discusses controversial issues within profeminism and examines the theoretical and political concerns raised by its modes of politics, the book is weighted towards to the more critically engaged perspectives within profeminism.

One point to note is that the choice of theorists changed throughout the writing of the book. Originally the work of Michael Kimmel was to be included: a writer and activist who has been a central figure in profeminist politics in the US. However, as the analysis developed, it became clear that Kimmel's work was paralleling the standpoints of several of the other writers chosen, which meant that including his work would have involved significant overlap with the other perspectives considered.

Theory

This discussion of profeminism employs new social movement theory inflexed by the insights of post-structuralist analysis. The book understands profeminism as a form of identity politics. As this volume attempts to show, profeminism is a politics that emphasises identity, lifestyle, morality, everyday life and culture. It is also a form of politics that develops standpoints and agendas through various assessments of the relationship between micro and macro forms of power, a hallmark of new social movement politics. Profeminism therefore displays the dimensions of a range of other contemporary collective movements. New social movement theorists have analysed the opportunities and complications that new forms of collective political activism have generated in contemporary cultures. A new social movement framework therefore helps flesh out the field of profeminist politics and supports the analysis of its potential effects across the field of gender relations.

While new social movement theory has been concerned to assess collective action in contemporary societies, post-structuralist philosophies have developed new insights around the key concepts associated with new social movements, namely subjectivity, power and resistance. While this study does not adopt post-structuralism's non-normative stance, it does recognise the importance of analysing the power-effects of knowledges that emerge around the concept of identity. Post-structuralist theory offers a range of theoretical tools to assess the effects of new formulations of identity. For post-structuralists like Foucault and Butler identity is constituted within diverse and shifting relationships of power. Identity, they suggest, does not precede culture but is constituted within social networks of power.

These theorists therefore suggest that defining identity ties subjectivity to a set of regulatory ideals. However, they contend that deconstructions of identities that unhinge identities from regulatory norms allow new possibilities around subjectivities to emerge. Subsequently it seems important to examine how the concept of identity operates in movement-politics. This volume pays special attention to the way in which the concept of men's identities is formulated within profeminist politics and traces the effects of deconstructions and reconstructions of identity within profeminism. Identity, of course, is a multi-faceted term and this study unpacks its dimensions to explore how profeminism frames, not only the concept of 'men' but other categories such as sexual difference, gendered experience, emotions and bodies.

Examining how aspects of profeminist identity politics intersect with the concept of power is also a key theme in this study. As already indicated this analysis of profeminism reflects the post-structuralist orientation towards examining the effect of knowledge-production around gendered categories and their relationships to power on profeminist modes of gender politics. Furthermore it highlights the profeminist analysis of micro-level forms of power on the constitution of inequality and considers how this has affected more modernist and structuralist analyses of systematic networks of power within profeminism. This framework is not the only possible analytical approach to men's gender-conscious politics. However it does provide a particular theoretical lens to examine some of the key areas of debate within profeminist politics. Furthermore it offers a way of focusing on the disruptive possibilities of profeminism within contemporary political contexts.

Structure of the book

The first part of the book outlines the context of profeminist politics. Chapter 2 briefly examines the emergence and dimensions of profeminist politics within contemporary contexts marked by shifts in gender relationships. Chapter 3 positions profeminism within the social and political contexts of late capitalist societies. It assesses the disorientating effects of these contexts on traditional forms of identities and, more specifically, on gendered identities. Chapter 4 reads profeminism through a new social movement framework to highlight the conceptual and political terrain of profeminist politics. Chapter 5 engages with the broader field of men's gender-conscious politics and examines the discourses that have been generated by alternative men's groups. The last chapter in this part of the book engages with feminist critiques of profeminist politics, particularly in relation to the concepts of identity and experience.

Part 2 of the book deals with profeminist perspectives and charts how different profeminist writers have engaged with the concepts of men's identities, power and resistance. It also examines how different writers have formulated profeminist politics in relationship to feminism and lesbian, gay and bisexual politics. Although there are overlaps between these writers' analyses of men and masculinities there are also significant areas of disagreement. Chapter 7 examines the work of Victor J. Seidler, chapter 8 concentrates on the work of John Stoltenberg and chapter 9 engages with Jeff Hearn's model of Critical Studies of Men. The final chapter assesses Raewyn Connell's framework of hegemonic and pluralistic masculinities. Although Connell has never identified as a profeminist, her work on masculinities has been extremely influential in terms of developing the field of profeminist theory and politics.

Part 1

Contexts

2 Men Doing Feminism

A contemporary movement?

> I've been digging *women* like never before, in new ways.
>
> Anon (*Men's Liberation* 1971: 8)

Profeminism is not a new phenomenon: however its contemporary form has a number of unique features that distinguish profeminist practice in late industrial societies from earlier forms of profeminist activity. This chapter examines the emergence and organisation of modern profeminism highlighting the 'newness' and specificity of contemporary profeminist politics. The chapter also charts some of the interrelationships between profeminist agendas and other forms of gendered politics. By mapping some of the features of profeminism and its affinities with other oppositional gendered communities the chapter commences the process of excavating the contours of profeminist politics, examined more fully in subsequent chapters.

Profeminism old and new

Feminism emerged as a movement concerned with women's inequality, standpoints and empowerment (see Spelman 1990). By the 1970s the Second Wave of feminism had developed a modern social movement forged through the energies of women. Although a diverse movement, Second Wave feminism often invoked the ideals of female solidarity and interconnectivity between women, notions which acted to frame feminism as a movement by women for women (Butler 1990; Rowbotham 1983; Rich 1976). Central to notions of female unity was the claim that women were connected through their experiences of oppression and their shared political interest in overthrowing systems of gender power.[1] Feminism's emphasis on securing women's gendered interests implied that men's power and masculine forms of dominance would have to be undermined (see for example

Dworkin 1974). Second Wave feminists therefore attacked the central sites of men's power, including gendered practices and institutions, and also masculine ideologies, ethics and values more generally (Eisenstein 1984; Tong 1989; Clough 1994).

Regardless of Second Wave feminism's emphasis on challenging men's power, from the 1960s a section of men openly declared solidarity with the feminist movement and supported women's struggle for gender justice (Strauss 1982; Clatterbaugh 1990; Kimmel and Mosmiller 1992; Messner 1997). Digby (1983b) has written about the peculiarity of the profeminist political standpoint. He notes the strangeness of profeminist men's affiliation with a feminist movement that seeks to undermine men's collective social power and individual gendered advantages. This narrative about the novelty of an oppressor identity joining in common cause with an oppressed identity has been implied by other profeminists (Pease 2000).

Yet history is littered with examples of members of dominant groups identifying with and participating in activism to reduce inequalities affecting subordinate groups. For example white Americans were active in the civil rights movement, middle class intellectuals have a history of aligning with the working class and heterosexuals have campaigned for the rights of gay, lesbian and bisexual people (Broad 2002). This type of political standpoint is therefore not new or particularly strange. As explained below, if profeminism has any novelty it lies in the degree to which men have deployed their identity as an organising principle for profeminist activism. Men involved in profeminism generally take the interrogation of their gendered identity as the starting point for feminist activism. The instantiation of a dominant identity as a basis for gender politics is one of profeminism's most distinctive political features.

The role that men's identity plays in contemporary profeminism is more easily identifiable if modern men's alignment with feminism is contrasted with earlier generations of men's support for women's equality. Men's affiliation with feminism is not peculiar to contemporary times. Historically feminism has had a number of male supporters and allies (Kimmel and Mosmiller 1992). American research has documented how, 'since the founding of the country' men have been involved in supporting women's struggle for equality (Kimmel and Mosmiller 1992: 2). These men were not leaders or even central figures in women's movements for equality but as Kimmel (1992) notes, historically men have been active in women's struggles.

For example men such as Thomas Paine, John Dewey and Ralph Waldo Emerson supported women's campaigns for property rights, equal access to education and suffrage (Kimmel and Mosmiller 1992). In his lecture *Woman* delivered to the Women's Rights Convention in Boston in 1855 Emerson illustrated the sometimes passionate nature of this support. During this lecture on women's suffrage Emerson declared: ' . . . Let the laws be purged of every barbarous impediment to women' (Emerson 1992: 219).

While historically a small number of men have embraced the ideal of greater equality between the sexes, the 1960s saw the emergence of a new kind of profeminist men's politics. Prior to the 1960s men who supported feminism tended to be isolated figures who gave their support to campaigns designed to improve women's social position. Although a few groups did exist such as the Men's League for Women's Suffrage, these groups tended to promote specific equality campaigns (see Kimmel and Mosmiller 1992: 32). In the late 1960s a new stage of profeminist activism emerged. Men in industrialised countries, such as the US, UK and Australia, organised profeminist men's groups that focused on the relationships between their identities, gender power and feminist theory and practice. Kimmel's (1998) historical research suggests that reflection on men's identities was also an element in earlier profeminist thinking. However this element was underdeveloped, marginal and limited in earlier profeminist activism and demonstrates little resemblance to the contemporary profeminist politicisation of men's identities.

For previous generations, normative forms of men's gender identity had been relatively unproblematic. Certainly, historically, gendered identities have undergone change and have at times been surrounded by anxieties about the 'proper roles' of men and women. However, as subsequent chapters will illustrate, such anxieties have been relatively mild in relation to contemporary concerns about men's normative gender identities. Before the Second Wave of feminism hegemonic models of male identity were viewed as normal; the standard by which others were judged and expected to aspire (see Rich 1976; Daly 1979; O'Brien 1983), or the standard to which others should be given access (see Kimmel and Mosmiller 1992). Men's identity was therefore framed as that of the 'generic human being' (Kimmel and Messner 1989: x). In contrast profeminism emerged as a form of politics that viewed men's identities as sites for political engagement in gender politics (see for example Hearn 1987; Connell 1995; Kimmel 1996).

Like earlier generations of profeminists, the men who developed post-1960s profeminism were concerned with supporting women's equality. However in contrast to men like Payne, Dewey and Emerson, contemporary profeminists have supported feminism by problematising traditional male identities. Traditional identities, such as the protector/provider model, reflect society's ideas about what kind of roles and ways of thinking are normal and natural for men. These identities have therefore been called normative male identities and are linked to the reiteration of gender power through men's everyday agency (Butler 1990). Theorists have argued that the practices and experiences of white, middle class, heterosexual men most clearly reflect the ideals of normative masculinity (e.g. Hoch 1979; Hearn and Collinson 1994; Kimmel 1994; Connell 1995). Much profeminist politics operates across this terrain of the normative and regulatory constitution of men's subjectivity and power.

The emphasis on identity in contemporary profeminist politics is connected to the particular cultural context within which this new form of gendered engagement by men emerged. The context of profeminism will be discussed in more detail in the next chapter. At this point it can be noted that the politics and oppositional discourses of feminism and the gay, lesbian and bisexual movement (LGBM) form a significant dimension of this cultural context. Feminism and the LGBM, played a central role from the 1960s in mapping the relationships between men, masculinity and gender/sexual oppression. These movements exposed the political 'nature' of men's identities.

Heavily influenced by these movements' critiques of the ideologies/discourses that produce men's identities, profeminists have viewed men's subjectivities as a central variable in the reproduction of women's inequality. They have also been concerned with mapping relationships of domination and subordination between masculinities. Profeminism's analysis of hegemonic masculinity, which reflects the normative ideals of manhood, has exposed how this ideal is discursively and materially constituted through the subordination of, for example, gay, working class and black masculinities (see e.g. Clatterbaugh 1990; Hearn and Collinson 1994; Connell 1995; Messner 1997).

Some contemporary profeminists have also been interested in the liberating potential of profeminist standpoints on men's identities (see Chapters 5 and 8). From the 1960s identity movements such as feminism, LGBM and the American civil rights movement, developed forms of social critique and political practices that explored the malleability of identity and its possible re-invention beyond established social definitions. Profeminism incorporated these movements' exploratory orientation towards identities into its political agenda.

Goldrick-Jones (2002: 31–34) has recorded the importance of ideas about the possible liberating effects of feminism on men's identities in the US context. She claims that the emergence of contemporary profeminism was generated by some men's sympathy towards feminist standpoints but she also highlights how notions of liberation from gender roles developed by feminists influenced men's interest in developing profeminist politics. Goldrick-Jones notes that:

> Many men [in the 1970s] were optimistic that, by supporting women's struggles against sexism, they would eventually discover much more fulfilling concepts of masculinity, just as many women were discovering much more empowering notions of femininity. By helping women to become more liberated, men might free themselves at the same time.
>
> (2002: 32)

However, other profeminist activists and writers have been critical of formulations of profeminist politics that operate around notions of men's liberation from oppressive gender roles. Several prominent profeminist writers have prioritised the category of men's power in terms of formulating models of profeminist theory and practice. These perspectives have developed complex links between identity and power and between the private and public domains of gender power (see Chapters 7, 9 and 10). Therefore notions of liberating men from normative gendered identities have been controversial as subsequent chapters will illustrate.

The emphasis on men's identity in profeminist politics is also reflected in the naming of the first national profeminist organisation which was called the National Organisation for Changing Men. Smaller profeminist groups also tend to take the relationship between identity and gender power as a starting point in their analysis of gender relationships. This concern with men's identities and its relation to gender power is reflected in profeminist scholarship which has prioritised a politics primarily concerned with understanding the categories of men, gender power and gender resistance across public and private arenas (for illustrations of the importance of identity in profeminism see Seidler 1992; Connell 1995; Stoltenberg 2000).

Therefore the categories of identity and power are central to profeminist politics and these concepts have been subjected to extensive theoretical debate within profeminism. As subsequent chapters will illustrate, different theorisations of identity and power engender particular forms of profeminist agendas and strategies. Much debate has emerged within profeminism around the form and effects of profeminist academic and political strategies.

This sketch of profeminism exposes how particular men, for the first time in history, have developed an ongoing political and theoretical agenda around the feminist and LGB movements' critiques of masculinity by using men's identities as a foundation for oppositional gender politics. As a whole, post-1960s profeminist groups allied with feminism but unlike earlier profeminist men these groups have carved out distinctive gendered concerns relating to men's identity.

The organisation of profeminism

Profeminism has organised and developed different forms of politics in different geographical contexts (see Strauss 1982; Hearn and Morgan 1990; Kimmel and Mosmiller 1992; Hearn and Hertta 2006; Hearn and Holmgren 2006). This section concentrates on the UK and US contexts. Clearly feminism and sexual politics has had a major influence on profeminism cross-culturally, by providing men with oppositional gendered knowledges, conceptual frameworks, political strategies and agendas of gender liberation. Furthermore, as already indicated, interrogations of masculinity have been a substantial element of Second and Third Wave feminism, and the gay movement has critiqued the effects of hegemonic masculinities on other sexualities.

Some profeminists have worked closely with feminists to develop knowledges around not only the relationship between men, masculinities and power but also gender relationships more broadly (see Chapter 9). Feminists have also engaged in collaborative politics with profeminists, for example through domestic violence campaigns and through the development of gender equity curricula in schools (see Kaufman 1993; Connell 2000: 210; Goldrick-Jones 2002). These have often been fruitful and as Part 2 illustrates have become commonplace in some strands of profeminism. Furthermore strands of profeminism have worked through issues relating to 'men doing feminism' in collaboration with feminists (see for example Hearn and Morgan 1990).

However specific collaborations between feminists and profeminists have led to particular feminists expressing deep reservations about the effects of 'men doing feminism' in public and private arenas (see Chapter 6 and also Spark 1994; Kaufman 1993; Goldrick-Jones 2002). Furthermore strands of profeminism have not been as open to developing collaborative strategies of resistance with feminists. Certain modes of profeminism appropriate aspects of feminist theory but argue that men need some degree of autonomy from feminism in order to engage effectively with interrogating and reforming their identities (see Chapter 8).

While some strands of profeminism have argued that profeminist men need to maintain some autonomy from feminism, some feminists have been highly concerned about men's move into feminist theory and politics. When profeminism began to emerge in a noticeable and visible form, particularly in profeminist men's academic work and more specifically in the development of 'Men's Studies', some feminists questioned men's new turn to feminism and gender politics (e.g. Canaan and Griffin 1990). Particular feminist critiques of men doing feminism have suggested that viewing profeminists as part of the feminist movement is problematic (see Chapter 6).

The main concerns that some feminists have raised in relation to profeminism revolve around issues of funding for research and women's centres (Canaan and Griffin 1990; Spark 1994). Furthermore some feminists have been worried about the possible dominating effects of men doing feminism (see Kimmel 1998 for discussion of this issue). The sincerity and commitment of profeminists have also been questioned, as have some of the political strategies developed by profeminists (Hester 1984; Jardine and Smith 1987; Modleski 1991; Moore 1998). Profeminism has responded to these concerns both analytically and politically as detailed in Part 2.

As already indicated profeminist men have had their own concerns about too close a connection with feminism. Some men have argued that too much involvement by feminists in profeminist politics may suppress distinctive profeminist perspectives from emerging (see Brod 1987; Seidler 1997; Pease 2000). A concern also emerged in some profeminists groups that feminism might be overly critical of men and masculinity (see e.g. Seidler 1997; Pease 2000)

Therefore profeminists have developed different models of politics. Small, local, profeminists groups have played a significant role in the development of the diverse strategies and standpoints that characterise profeminism. Since its emergence in the 1960s profeminism has tended to remain a fluid, decentralised, multi-faceted form of politics. Profeminist groups have developed strategies for reforming men and reforming gender relations more broadly, and have also, in some geographical contexts such as Finland, organised within the state and governmental machinery through the Subcommittee on Men's Issues. The subcommittee is made up of men and women who are experts, activists or interested in gender issues; some of its members are profeminists (Hearn and Hertta 2006).

In terms of the numbers of men involved in profeminist activism, membership of actual profeminist groups remains small and like other identity groups, profeminist groups are prone to fragmentation (Gamson 1995). Larger profeminist groups tend to be more concentrated in urban areas and have a broader membership (Goldrick-Jones 2002).

National organisations have also emerged alongside small groups and individual commitments by men to anti-sexist practices. Given the associations of masculinity with power, control and hierarchy some profeminists have tended to be wary of developing structured organisations with formalised procedures (see Goldrick-Jones 2002). To some extent this reflects the concerns of some feminists that hierarchal and formal organisational structures may mirror masculinist institutions. However more structured organisations have developed with centralised decision-making procedures and executive committees, such as the National Organization for Men against Sexism (NOMAS) and the White Ribbon Campaign (WRC) discussed below (see Goldrick-Jones 2002).

The first and only national profeminist organisation in the USA, which was named the National Men's Organization, formed in the United States at the beginning of the 1980s. This organisation was renamed the National Organization for Changing Men (NOCM) in 1983. It developed out of a number of *Men and Masculinity* conferences held in the 1970s, which were originally organised by men taking women's studies courses at the University of Tennessee. NOCM was renamed NOMAS in 1992. The organisation's newsletter is called *Brother.*

The most well known profeminist men's group in Britain is probably the Achilles Heel Collective which formed alongside the publication of the *Achilles Heel* magazine in 1978. Many of the founding members of this group were originally involved in socialist politics and a movement called *Red therapy* which attempted to modify alternative forms of therapy such as Gestalt to include issues of class, race and gender inequality (Seidler 1991b). The Achilles Heel Collective developed a much looser organisational style compared with NOMAS, which has a designated spokesperson and a steering committee.

In Australia, Men Against Sexism (MAS) organised nationally and set up the Australian Men's Network. MAS was superseded by Men Against Sexual Assault (MASA) which tried to organise a national campaign against sexual violence towards women in Australia in the early 1990s (Goldrick-Jones 2002: 143–44). In Canada profeminists organised a national White Ribbon Campaign, discussed further below, to highlight and prevent violence towards women. These national organisations and campaigns have situated themselves as responses to feminism's challenges to men to reform their identities.

As such they have provided a focal point for profeminist politics and the profeminist community. More broadly the myriad of autonomous profeminist groups address a range of issues and formulate different political agendas and practices. For example some groups have organised ongoing campaigns around specific issues such as reducing male violence against women, whereas others engage in more self-exploratory activities through conscious-raising and therapy (see Goldrick-Jones 2002). Overall male profeminism is composed of a number of independent profeminist groups, friendship circles and individual men's alignment with feminism. Internets sites, pamphlets, magazines, journals and books facilitate communication within the profeminist community, articulate the movement's philosophy and form an arena of debate within profeminist politics.

In terms of its organisation within academia, profeminism has tried to promote and develop studies of masculinities. Divisions again have emerged around the way studies of men should be carved out within academia. Some profeminists have developed 'men's studies' courses, while others have tried to integrate with feminism by locating studies of masculinities with gender studies (see Chapter 9).

Regardless of these differences between profeminist academics, profeminism's influence in the area of gender studies has been significant. Academia has been saturated by books analysing men and masculinities. As MacInness (1998: 1) has noted 'it seems like every man and his dog is writing a book about masculinity'. Writers such as Connell, Hearn, Kimmel, Kaufman, Seidler and Stoltenberg have become leaders in this relatively new, yet now substantial and burgeoning field of research. Several feminist writers such as Lynne Segal (e.g. 1999) and Faludi (1999) have been key contributors to this field. Journals such as *Men and Masculinities* and the *Journal of Men's Studies* have supported academic discussion and debate among profeminists. Feminist journals such the *Journal of Gender Studies* have also disseminated profeminist studies of gender and perspectives. Sage Publications runs a men and masculinities series (Messner 1997).

Like feminists, profeminists have been concerned about the concept of 'difference.' Feminism has been dominated by debates about the significance of differences between women for feminist organisation and theory. One of the critical issues in feminism has been claims that feminism has excluded certain categories of women, such as lesbians, working class women and women from non-white ethnic/racial groups or nationalist groups (Butler 1990).

Similarly profeminism has been concerned that profeminist groups and organisations have been dominated by white, middle class, heterosexual men who may be reproducing a white, middle class, heterosexual standpoint and political practice. High profile profeminist organisations and scholars have therefore been keen to examine differences between men, and some activists have argued that profeminism needs to be responsive to and reflect the perspectives of different categories of men. Moreover some profeminists have been eager to 'reach out' to categories of men who do not participate in profeminism to prevent profeminism from becoming a collection of predominantly white, middle class, heterosexual organisations and groups. Although it should be noted that gay men have been more attracted to joining NOMAS compared with other groups of non-hegemonic men (Goldrick-Jones 2002).

Visibility, scale and influence

The decentralised and fragmented nature of profeminist politics means that its influence on men generally is difficult to gauge. Whitehead (2002: 67) claims that there is evidence that across 'all four continents' men are recognising the political issues that surround their gender identity. He observes that 'more men, and not only white American males, appear prepared to critically reflect on themselves as masculine subjects in the postmodern, postindustrial age' and have been 'engaging in ways of being that are closely aligned with feminist agendas . . . '

Certainly profeminism has had an impact on some men in late capitalist societies. However only very small numbers of men have been involved in the national organisations. For example MASA organised a national gathering of MASA groups in 1992 and only about eighteen men attended (Goldrick-Jones 2002). The Boston chapter of NOMAS has around 10–12 members and around 80 people on their public e-list (NOMAS Boston 2006).

Despite the diversity and modest scale of profeminist activism, profeminists have been able to organise a number of public campaigns with differing degrees of success. The MASA, Men Can Stop Rape marches held in 1990, 1991, 1992 and 1993 in Melbourne, attracted between 200 and 500 men (Goldrick-Jones 2002: 145–46). The Canadian White Ribbon Campaign generated substantially more impact. This campaign emerged in response to the murder of 14 women engineers in Ecole Polytechnique, Montreal, in 1989 by anti-feminist Marc Lepine (Connell 1993: 6; Kaufman 1993). This campaign drew considerable media attention and, within six weeks of the campaign, one hundred thousand men across Canada wore a white ribbon (Goldrick-Jones 2002: 69). The campaign also had considerable fund-raising success. As the campaign developed, more formal procedures emerged leading to the formation of the White Ribbon Foundation (WRF) (Goldrick-Jones 2002: 70–71).

Smaller profeminist groups also engage in a range of political activities such as co-counselling and anti-violence initiatives, but on a much smaller scale. Again it is difficult to assess the impact of these campaigns at local levels. Less formal connections with the profeminist movement, through readership of national journals, certainly indicate higher levels of participation than, for example, the MASA campaigns. For example the profeminist magazine *Changing Men* achieved a readership of 6,000 in its final year of publication. *Changing Men* folded in the 1990s. By comparison the non-feminist mythopoetic publications *Men's Council Journal* and *Wingspan: Journal of the Male Spirit* had readerships of 10,000 and 150,000 in 1994 (Goldrick-Jones 2002: 173).

However profeminists have been able to impact on policy making networks. For example the EU has funded the European Research Network on Men in Europe that examines 'the social problem and social problematisation of men and masculinities' (European Commission 2006). The research network is comprised of members of the research group, Critical Research on Men in Europe or CROME established in 1999. CROME has brought together researchers, both men and women, from across Europe to work collaboratively on the study of practices of men including policy development (Hearn and Pringle with members of CROME 2006). Profeminists in collaboration with feminists have also tried to influence UN discussions on gender equality (Connell 1995: 265–66). Other international organisations have also been influenced by profeminists. For example, Kaufman has had high profile involvement in Amnesty International's campaign to stop violence against women.

The above outline has exposed profeminism's contemporary form and its central organisational features. Understanding why this particular form of politics emerged and expanded in the post-1960s period is a more complex enterprise because it demands not only an analysis of the impact of gender/sexual politics on some men but also requires an examination of the cultural context of contemporary profeminism that has influenced modern identities. The next chapter explores the political, social and cultural forces that have shaped profeminism in its contemporary form. Moreover it examines the changing contours of identity constitution in late industrialised societies and examines how political, social and cultural change has affected men's identities.

3 Profeminism, Masculinity and Social Change

Contemporary culture and identity

> We need to perceive ourselves in our own narratives.
>
> John Stoltenberg (2000: xvii)

A body of social and political theory has suggested that late industrial societies have undergone a range of economic, social and cultural changes from the 1960s. Analysts claim that one of the main outcomes of these changes has been that a new significance has been assigned to identity in contemporary Western societies. Identities in modern societies have become sites of scrutiny, debate and reconfiguration. The category of identity has also increasingly acted as a foundation for oppositional political movements. Men's identities have not been insulated from the social changes that have increased the importance of identity in contemporary societies. This chapter explores the general social changes that have emerged to generate interest in contemporary identities and explores the more specific changes that have promoted new debates and forms of gendered politics around men's identities.

Social change, politics and identity

Alberto Melucci (1989: 178) has argued that one of the most important and prized values in industrialised societies is the 'freedom to be'. This particular formulation of freedom revolves around the concept of identity and usually involves the desire to define one's identity and way of life in opposition to social codes and to the social categorisations imposed on specific groups. Melucci (1989; 1996a) and other theorists have exposed identity as a crucial site of struggle in modern societies. (Habermas 1981; 1989; Foucault 1982; Laclau and Mouffe 1985; Young 1990; Haraway 1991). Collective political action in advanced industrialised societies has increasingly been marked by concerns about the relationship between identities, power and social justice. A broad range of contemporary political groups have forged forms of politics based around refusing and contesting the boundaries and proscriptions of traditional definitions of identities.

For example, the LGBM and feminism have challenged traditional definitions of gender and sexuality. These movements have also questioned ascribed ways of living out gender and sexual identities and have explored alternative lifestyles and ethical frameworks (see Daly 1979; Weeks 1986). Feminism and the LGBM therefore struggle to reinvent gender and sexual identities beyond existing social ideologies or discourses. This approach to identities has not been confined to gendered/sexual politics. There are a range of contemporary political groups that contest modalities of power that subjugate certain identity groups and also challenge society's definitions of members of those groups (for overviews see Tilley 1978; Melucci 1989; Tarrow 1994; Della Porta and Dani 1998).

Profeminism, as the last chapter highlighted, also operates across the terrain of identity and power. Of course profeminism differs from feminism and LGB politics because it takes an oppressor or dominant identity as its organising point. However, this form of politics has formulated a set of concerns about identity that reflect the identity concerns of a range of other contemporary social movements. It is therefore possible to situate profeminism within the more general politics of identity that marks advanced industrialised societies.

Theorists have traced the emergence of this relatively new political concern with identities to the 1960s. Several writers claim that capitalist societies underwent a number of social changes that generated the conditions for a range of NSMs highlighting and organising around the concept of a shared yet problematic identity (see Laraña, Johnson and Gusfield 1994; Della Porta and Dani 1998 for overviews). The rest of this section examines the relationships between post-1960s social change, identity and identity politics and explores how these social changes stimulated identity movements. It also investigates the impact of these changes on contemporary gendered identities. Against this background, the following sections examine explicitly how post-1960s social changes have impacted on men's identities and subsequently stimulated a new politics of masculinity of which contemporary profeminism forms a part.

Unstable identities, de-traditionalisation and gender identity

Giddens (1990; 1991; 1992; 1999) has developed a very general theory of the social changes that have amplified the importance of personal and group identities in advanced industrial societies. Much of Giddens' (e.g. 1990; 1991; 1992; 1999) recent writing has been concerned with mapping the different effects of traditional, modern and advanced industrial societies on human identity. Giddens develops a theory of de-traditionalisation as a central force in the production of critical social reflections on identity and the formation of identity movements. Giddens' de-traditionalisation thesis connects directly to notions about the decoupling of men's identity from its traditional ideological and institutional anchors through processes of modernisation. The next two sections suggest that Giddens' theory of de-traditionalisation identifies important factors that have impacted on men's identity in contemporary societies but insist that his theorisation of social changes around identities needs to be reworked to take account of the complexity of the present field of gender relationships within which men's identities are located.

Giddens (1990; 1991; 1992) claims that in traditional societies the individual's actions were guided by habit, custom, long established social mores and institutional arrangements. Traditional ways of life, he argues, gave individuals a coherent life narrative and a sense of a secure identity. Therefore in traditional societies, according to Giddens, identity was not a matter that required extensive reflection by individuals. Traditional societies 'held up' a model of identity for different social categories or groups and individuals identified with these models without much reflection. The space for personal decision-making and lifestyle choices was therefore highly limited in societies wherein tradition acted as a guide to action.

Giddens (1994) argues that in modern societies, which he believes emerged with the Enlightenment, traditional ways of life were subjected to scrutiny. However the Enlightenment's faith in science and progress meant that the development of new collectivist institutions such as the welfare state and employment organisations provided people with rules, ideals and guidelines about their place in society and buttressed them from risk and decision-making.

According to Giddens (1991; 1992), the constitution of identities in contemporary societies has changed radically. His thesis is that in advanced industrial societies or what he terms 'high modernity', the impact of globalisation has changed the way people construct their identities. For Giddens, globalisation undermines established traditions and institutions. For example, it erodes cultural boundaries and decreases the power of national governments. These processes destabilise traditions and open up local cultures to a range of pluralistic ideas imported from outside of their boundaries. Furthermore, Giddens argues, globalisation requires coordination across time and space. Expert systems, he suggests, fill this function and these systems intervene in more and more areas of life in high modernity. This process again undermines tradition as a guide to behaviour and leads to a myriad of social sites becoming subject to the rational interventions of experts and professionals.

Expert systems therefore draw what were once areas of life based around tradition into the orbit of social enquiry (Giddens 1990; 1991; 1992). Furthermore, in late modernity the old collectivist institutions that gave people the ideal of, for example lifelong employment, have rescinded and no longer provide stable ideologies through which people can locate their social identities. Giddens (1990; 1991; 1992; 1999) claims that these shifts again undermine tradition as a guide to action in late industrial societies.

As established norms become increasingly opened up to critique, Giddens (1991) claims that institutions such as the family and sexuality are no longer structured by tradition but must be justified through rational argumentation. The social norms that surround identities in high modernity have, he believes, become sites of intense debate and contestation leading to the development of alternative ways of living.

Furthermore, in the social conditions of globalisation people become 'dis-embedded' from traditional ways of life and have to try to constitute their identities within cultures characterised by a plurality of knowledges and fewer traditional anchors of identity. Individuals, Giddens (1991: 5) claims, are 'forced to negotiate lifestyle choices [from] among a diversity of options'. In this cultural environment, the social self becomes 'a reflexive project', for which the individual is responsible (1991: 192).

Therefore at the social and everyday level Giddens (1991) claims that individuals and groups, having become dislocated from tradition, are now free to make their own decisions about their lifestyle. Freedom from longstanding expectations about people's identities expands lifestyle and ethical choices. Faced with different possibilities in terms of identity constitution, Giddens (1991: 70) maintains that moderns increasingly have to consider the way that they live their lives and the personal choices that they make. He (1991) contends that we are now in a period of increased 'reflexivity' on the self and this reflexivity has spread to all areas of life in high modernity.

The increased 'reflexivity', that marks contemporary society, according to Giddens, has been driven forward by social movements such as feminism, and he maintains that these relatively new movements intensify the questioning of identities by formulating alternative lifestyles and ethical frameworks. For Giddens, the social conditions of late modernity make identity a site for the development of 'dialogic democracy' across a range of social inequities and this is the territory on which identity movements operate. Overall Giddens argues that the de-traditionalisation of society has stimulated a new politics around group identities.

Other theorists have mapped the politics of identity in late modernity through alternative frameworks. For example, Habermas (1981) views NSMs, including identity movements, as a consequence of increased instrumental rationalisation reflected in the increase in the social application of means-end solutions to ethical issues. Habermas therefore suggests that NSMs are 'border campaigns' against the increased rationalisation of the private and civil spheres of society. Habermas's theory therefore overlaps to some extent with Giddens' recognition of the emergence of expert systems. Foucault (1982) theorises the new politics around identity as resistances to the normative categorisations of identity often produced by modern social scientific knowledges. Both theorists expose the power structures of late modernity as more insidious than Giddens' theory of modernisation suggests. Foucault's theory in particular, as will be explained shortly exposes how contemporary identities are saturated with power.

While theoretical disagreement marks the study of identity movements, most theorists in the area suggest that moderns' sense of identity has become less stable and a site where forms of power are contested (Habermas 1981; Foucault 1982; Laclau and Mouffe 1995; Melucci 1996a). Giddens' work therefore marks fundamental shifts in identities, analysed by other theorists and his work is helpful in the sense that it exposes the increased social space for experimentation with identities. Giddens exposes the increased interrogation of identities in contemporary societies and ties this process to important variables that have marked the post-1960s period. His work can also be applied in a way that highlights significant trends in the development of identity movements such as profeminism, considered in the next section.

However Giddens does not provide an adequate framework for examining the complexity of the new interrogations of masculinity or the gendered identity movements that operate within this interrogatory space. Competing theorisations of contemporary identities, discussed in later sections of this chapter expose Giddens' under-theorisation of the continuing interconnection of identity and power in high modernity. More specifically, Giddens unhinges identity from tradition in high modernity too sharply, especially in the case of gender and this has implications for understanding the changes and politics that have emerged around men's identities in late industrial societies. De-traditionalisation, reflexivity and the incursion of expert systems into the private sphere are concepts that help highlight the forces of change that have produced the contemporary terrain of men's identity politics. However these concepts need to be reworked to take account of the continuing operation of normative and traditional forms of gender power on the field of gender politics, sexuality and identity.

Gender, identity and change

Giddens is certainly correct to pinpoint that identity politics arises from a loosening of tradition and his claim that identity movements target and undermine traditional definitions of subjugated identity groups seems reflective of the agendas of these movements. However Giddens does not recognise adequately the continuing role that traditional gendered and sexual discourses play in the formulation of identity movements and in the reconstitution of identities in contemporary societies. As explained below, he fails to identify the interconnections between traditional constitutions of identities and the processes he examines such as social change and interrogations of identities. He also fails to recognise how deeply traditional discourses about identities impact on individual and movement experimentation with subjectivity, an issue discussed in the next section. This has implications for any understanding of contemporary gender politics.

Giddens' neglect of the continuing effects of tradition across the terrain of gender relationships is clearly visible on closer examination of his theory of 'pure relationships' in the private sphere: a theory that reflects his more general propositions. The concept of 'pure relationships' emerges from a theorisation of contemporary heterosexual relationships. This conceptualisation of gendered relationships impacts directly on the analysis of contemporary masculinities. Giddens (1992) claims that under the conditions of high modernity, the patriarchal nuclear family has been replaced by the development of different relationships between married and cohabiting partners and children. He argues that the development of expert systems in late modernity has given rise to a mental health system and psychotherapeutic ideologies that have generated discourses of individual fulfilment and 'growth' in personal relationships. This new focus on personal happiness and development, Giddens claims, eroded the old narratives of marriage that were based around the ideals of the patriarchal family and supported the ideal of lifelong commitments and obligations by marriage partners.

According to Giddens, these shifts led to the development of the 'pure relationship' in heterosexual intimacy and monogamous heterosexual partnerships. Individual autonomy, he maintains, becomes prized over obligation and commitment. Individuals in high modernity stay in relationships for as long as their needs are being met, he contends, and if their needs cannot be met they separate. Furthermore, 'pure relationships' are not based on the old regulatory ideals of the patriarchal family but are reformulated by Giddens as negotiated arenas where individuals modify their relationships to achieve the autonomy and self-fulfilment of both parties. This representation of contemporary heterosexual relationships suggests that men and women's familial roles have fundamentally changed.

Certainly marriage and romantic relationships have changed and have become more liberal in recent decades. However, Giddens ignores the full dynamics of contemporary heterosexual relationships. An excellent and much needed research article by Gross (2005) disputes the validity of Giddens' claims about the de-traditionalisation of intimate heterosexual relationships. Gross exposes the continuing influence of traditional ideals about men and women's roles within relationships. He claims that while divorce is on the rise and women's employment and personal freedom have expanded, traditional ideals continue to influence heterosexual relationships. Gross provides survey data that suggests that traditional patriarchal beliefs and practices remain strong, from old style conceptions of patriarchal romantic love to the dominance and power of men in contemporary marriages and relationships.

Gross (2005: 299) states that while social changes have had a liberalising effect on heterosexual relationships and social movements have developed 'alternative imageries' of intimate relationships, 'motherhood, domesticity, and kin-work' remain crucial elements in relationships for women. Furthermore many women and men 'believe that it is the duty of a husband to financially provide for his wife', with many women continuing to 'cling to the ideal of intensive mothering' (298).

Feminists have also exposed how the so-called autonomy and fulfilment delivered by the loosening of social stigmas around martial breakdown and divorce have often driven women into poverty and have placed women in a position where they are not only providing all or the majority of the physical and emotional requirements of children but also shouldering most of the financial burden of children (National Congress of Women 1992; Folbre 1994).

In terms of gender, societies change, but traditional discourses about men and women continue to constitute gendered subjects and gender practices in traditional ways, albeit in more liberal and ideologically pluralistic social environments. This means that reflexivity interacts with traditional gendered frameworks. Furthermore, in relation to gender identities reflexivity is for many people, faced with the practicalities of life, such as earning an income, getting children to school on time and caring for family members, still limited. As studies of gender suggest many people continue to conform to the hegemonic ideals of gender across a range of behaviours (see e.g. Connell 2000; Gross 2005). Domestic violence, female poverty, sexual double standards and gender discrimination all continue in the era of de-traditionalisation despite the increasing social scrutiny of identity categories, relationships and practices.

Moreover, the prolonged and intense struggles for gender and sexual justice by feminism and the LGBM highlight the spaces that have opened in late modernity for political resistance against inequalities, but they also expose the tenacity and depth of traditional forms of power in relation to subjugated identities. Feminist and LGB explorations of gender power continue to expose how insinuated and insidious those forms of power remain in contemporary society (see for example Weeks 2000; Ashe 2006d). Studies have suggested that contemporary subjects are thoroughly saturated with different and cross-cutting modalities of power (Foucault 1980a; Butler 1990). The conclusion then is that societies can undergo substantial social change but gendered and other inequalities while loosening in some respects, can become modified and reproduced in new conditions (see Walby 1990; Hearn 1999).

The next section qualifies Giddens' de-traditionalisation thesis to examine how post-1960s social changes have continued to impact on men's identities. It examines the social transformations around men's identities, the expansion of expert systems on the field of gender politics and the increasing critique and reflexivity around men's identities but it also exposes how these changes have intersected with traditional and normative ideas about the subjectivities, rights and obligations of gendered and sexual subjects. It then frames profeminism as a movement that seeks to extend reflexivity around men's identities within complex networks of gender power.

De-traditionalisation, tradition, reflexivity and men's identities

The period of late modernity that Giddens theorises was certainly marked by changes driven by globalisation, the liberalisation of the private spheres of life and increased scrutiny around identities. In the 1960s and 1970s scrutiny surrounded women's identities, alternative sexualities and the identities of a range of ethnic groups. By the 1980s and 1990s masculinity had became one of the most scrutinised and debated identities in advanced industrial societies. This scrutiny of male identity was generated by the macro-level social changes that started to emerge from the 1960s and more specific changes in gender discussed below.

Feminism has been the central movement pushing critical forms of reflexivity around gender identities. Feminism is both an effect of recent social shifts in late modernity and, as Giddens (1992) notes, has also been a movement that has deepened the interrogation of identities. Feminism has focused scrutiny on men's identities and the structures of power that validate those identities and that support men's dominant social positions. As noted earlier, feminism's interrogation of gender has challenged natural and functional justifications for gender arrangements. Feminism has also challenged male values of militarism, aggression and rationality (Rich 1976; Daly 1976; O'Brien 1983). The concrete gains of feminism, for example in the form of equality laws, have combined with feminism's critique of gendered identities in ways that have encouraged the development of a problematic around traditional gender identities.

As outlined earlier, LGB politics have also targeted scrutiny on the hegemonic ideals of masculinities (see Weeks 1977; 1986). Feminism and LGB politics developed alternative ways of living and thinking about sexuality and gender. Both movements have not only interrogated normative gender identities and heterosexuality but have also explored and exposed the fluidity of the concept of gender. The antagonisms that feminism and gay politics have created around sexuality and gender have combined and intertwined with specific social changes to destabilise the ideological and institutional anchors of traditional male identities and roles in the last four decades.

Both movements 'pulled' men's gendered identities into the arena of political discourses. These social movements challenged traditional readings of gender by de-naturalising gender and undermining claims that gender identities are biological states located in the private sphere of personal identity. Feminism and gay politics have exposed masculinities as thoroughly political. The de-naturalisation, de-traditionalisation and politicisation of men's identities has meant that it is now both a political issue and open to political debate.

However the social changes that emerged alongside these movements intensified the discursive struggles around men's identities. The dimensions of the social changes that have affected contemporary masculinity have been outlined by a number of other writers; therefore they will only be summarised in this section (see e.g. Brittan 1989; MacInnes 1998; Chapman 1998; Faludi 1999). During the 1980s and 1990s commentators, especially in the UK, North America and Australia, suggested that modern men were undergoing a crisis of identity as social change and the impact and effects of feminism were increasingly affecting traditional male roles. The political differences of writers examining these changes produced very different accounts of the causes and effects of post-1960s gender changes on men's social position and roles (compare Lyndon 1992 with Hearn 1992; 1999).

The changes in men's roles during this period were generally viewed as linked to improvements in women's position. The rise in female employment, feminism and the liberalisation of social attitudes towards sexuality and divorce were all linked to changes in men's traditional institutional roles. For example, the global restructuring of the economy and the impact of the feminist movement meant that by the 1980s the contemporary workplace could no longer be viewed as the preserve of men: an arena fundamental to the production of the traditional masculine role of breadwinner (Tolson 1977).

Increases in divorce rates and the development of alternative family forms also impacted on men's traditional roles as fathers in the nuclear family. As these changes became manifest more plural representations of masculinity began to emerge. The media were instrumental in producing a range of identities for men. For example, as the introduction to this volume indicated, the media produced the ideal of the 'new man' who pushed prams, engaged in extensive grooming and was generally 'in touch' with his feminine side. He was quickly replaced in the UK by another media invention, the 'new lad'. The 'new lad' was a beer swilling playboy and generally rejected the 'sissy stuff' associated with the 'new man' (see Moore 1998; Mort 1998 for further commentary).

The media 'play' with men's identities illustrates the way that social and ideological changes around men's identities increased the reflexivity that Giddens talks about on masculinities. This was particularly evident in the notion that masculinity was in crisis and required societal investigation. Certainly, historical studies (Kimmel 1987b; Roper and Tosh 1991) expose masculinity as an arena of reflection and debate in previous eras. However, the contemporary reflection on masculinity has been far more intense, reflected in the explosion of debate around masculinities in the 1990s.

Social and ideological changes affecting men's identities gave rise to reflexivity on a range of issues relating to men's roles, subjectivities and failures. For example, society and individuals reflected on issues such as what makes a good lover, good partner, good father, good son and so on. There was also significant reflexivity on the limitations of the traditional 'male role' in terms of men's emotional capacities, orientation towards violence and relationships with children and women.

Furthermore the greater intervention of what Giddens calls 'expert systems' drew issues relating to men's reproductive capacity and anatomy into the political field, generating new debates and reflection on, for example, the effect of reproductive technologies on men. The media regularly peddled the idea that reproduction technologies, such as artificial insemination, were making men biologically redundant. Other expert systems also emerged around men's financial responsibilities to their children outside of traditional marriages. For example new government agencies such as the Child Support Agency (CSA), set up in Britain through the Child Support Act passed in 1991 by a conservative administration, rationally calculated the amount of child support men should pay to their children (see also Hearn 1998c). This type of intervention on the domestic and familial terrain illustrates the restructuring of familial responsibilities through expert systems. The 'intrusion' of these systems into arenas of private life therefore opened gender stereotypes, norms and responsibilities to greater public debate.

The general concerns around men's identities during this period were also translated into psycho-analytic and psychological frameworks. Following Giddens' logic the shifts in the workplace, the family and in the ideologies around intimacies pushed forward by gender politics and social changes, generated a range of self-help books for men, new male-centred therapeutic practices and spiritualist movements that developed alternative or modified readings of masculinity. The production of these kinds of discourses suggests that social forces were pushing individuals towards seeing men's identities as more malleable and pluralistic, and also more the responsibility of the individual rather than a consequence of pre-given models of 'male' subjectivity. The new and less predictable conditions for the production of masculinities, represented for example in increased marital break-up, therefore intensified reflexivity around men's identities at the personal and subjective levels. However, as Chapter 4 will illustrate, these discourses retained and reworked many traditional ideas about men and women's subjectivities.

Therefore reflexivity has emerged around men's identities in contemporary societies but it has not been 'discursively bounded' within the new pluralistic, de-traditionalised structures of high modernity. Rather it operated and continues to operate at the intersection of oppositional and traditional discourses. Regulative, conservative and anti-feminist discourses were deployed and modified within the new field of reflexivity around men's identities. These kinds of discourses were produced through the media, social commentators and the new men's groups and movements that began to emerge in the 1970s and expanded in the 1990s (see Chapter 5). The undermining of men's roles in the workplace and the family, and the new debates around reproductive technologies were viewed, especially by conservative writers, as creating or intensifying a number of social problems such as higher levels of male exploitation, suicide, depression, alcoholism and crime, especially youth crime (compare e.g. Campbell 1993; Murray 1995).

Men's groups have developed within this discursive arena wherein the ontological security of men's traditional identities have been questioned and disrupted but also reproduced through societal and political discourses. Anti-feminist groups and men's groups have continued to develop agendas designed to defend men's traditional social positions, rights and roles (see Clatterbaugh 1990; Messner 1997). Spiritualist discourses have also continued to develop around the concept of masculinity. Some of these discourses have attempted to modify traditional discourses around men's identities in modern conditions (e.g. Bly 1990). Spiritualist men's groups have incorporated symbols of masculinity from other cultures and combined these symbols with older regulative ideals about masculinity such as the idea of a masculine essence or core (Hagan 1992; Kimmel 1998a; 1998b). Other groups have continued to produce what have been called liberationist agendas for men. These groups cultivate the idea that women have been winning the 'sex war' and this has resulted in the virtual 'defeat of the male sex' (Heartfield, 2002).

As already indicated, profeminism emerged in the 1960s against a background of social and political change. Since its emergence it has continued to develop within a culture increasingly concerned with identities and criss-crossed with competing discourses around changes in men's identities. Profeminism has employed feminist and LGB discourses to develop forms of reflexivity around the category of men. The increased ontological insecurity around men's identity has therefore been a factor in the continued development of new groups of men organising politically around their gendered identities.

However the direction of men's reflexivity on their identities emerges from a complex web of personal biographies, personal experiences, class background, familial background, relationships with women, exposure to feminism and experiences within men's groups and organisations. Most commentators view exposure to feminism and feminist women as a key motivator for men's profeminism; it is one of the main influences cited in profeminist men's biographical accounts of the reasons that they became feminists (see Stoltenberg 1990; Christian 1994; Digby 1998; Pease 2000).

Some personal biographies identify other motivators such as men's individual experiences of the 'dark side' of masculinities (Awkward 1999). As the Achilles Heel Collective illustrates, profeminism has also evolved out of men's involvement in other forms of left-wing politics (Seidler 1991b; Connell 1995). Therefore feminism interacting with broader social changes and other factors such as men's personal biographies has encouraged a small number of men to explore the possibilities for changing men and society in ways that oppose traditional gendered frameworks.

Subsequent chapters expose the problems that emerge from profeminism's operation within a culture that is changing but still enmeshed in networks of gender power. At this point it can be highlighted that identities that engage in feminist struggle in contemporary contexts are constituted through networks of power that they seek to oppose. Post-structuralist theory for example suggests that the concept of men is in effect a social constitution rather than a prediscursive identity (Butler 1990). Post-structuralist accounts of gender resistance therefore suggest that even an agency that seeks to refuse normative identities is still saturated in power (Butler 1990). If identity is viewed as a product of society rather than given biologically, then the agency of any identity will be interconnected with the social forces that have constituted it. In profeminism this connection to the normative structuring of identity is complicated further by the dominant position of men. The different strategies that profeminists have deployed will also affect how these issues emerge within its politics. The next chapter examines profeminist politics in relation to other contemporary social movements to flesh out the dimensions of the new forms of political activism that have emerged around issues of identity, power and resistance.

4 Profeminism and Identity Politics

Masculinity, new times, new politics

> ... buy yourself some flowers and let the florist know they are for you. Individual action for profeminist men.
>
> (Wernette, Acacia and Scherfenberg 1992: 428)

Previous chapters have shown how contemporary profeminism fuses men's identity with feminist politics to produce a political subjectivity that engages in new forms of political antagonisms around the concepts of masculinity and gender power. This chapter explores the general style of profeminist antagonisms around men's identities, which according to various theories of contemporary politics can also be viewed as having elements of 'newness' in terms of profeminism's emphasis on identity, lifestyle choices, symbolic networks and civil society. These features of profeminist politics mean that it operates on a similar political terrain to other contemporary social movements.

However, as the introduction indicated, profeminists have developed different theoretical and political models to challenge men's traditional identities and also broader relationships of gender inequality. Therefore, while profeminism has incorporated the new political concerns associated with contemporary movements, strands of profeminism have continued to highlight the importance of maintaining a more traditional focus on institutional and macro-level forms of power. What is perhaps most interesting is the way that some strands of profeminism have interrelated more traditional forms of politics with political concerns associated with new social movements. This chapter examines the dimensions of new social movements. Part 2 examines more closely how new forms of political practice interconnect with more traditional forms of activism in profeminist politics.

A substantial literature has emerged that has examined the contours of contemporary social movements of which identity movements form a subset. This chapter reads profeminist politics through this literature to expose the distinct approach to thinking about collective political engagement that profeminism shares with other contemporary movements. The chapter assesses the implications of profeminism's broad approach to gender politics in terms of NSM and other contemporary political theories and outlines the constellation of issues that emerge around profeminism's application of the NSM styles of political engagement. Later chapters expose how new styles of political engagement interlink with more traditional forms of politics within profeminism.

Profeminism: a new social movement?

Whitehead (2002: 67) counsels against applying NSM analysis to profeminism. He claims that it is inaccurate to view men's 'profeminist engagements as representing a social movement and argues that profeminism is more reflective of a loose coalition of interests'. According to Whitehead then, classifying profeminism as a social movement is problematic because of its organisational features. However this definitional difficulty is not exclusive to profeminism and theorists have debated whether other forms of politics that are extremely decentralised can be viewed as actual political movements or should be viewed as political networks or counter-cultures (see Della Porta and Dani 1998; Buechler 2000 for discussions). Framing NSMs in this way suggests that effective political action is marked by the development of structured political agendas and formal organisational processes by movements.

Other commentators highlight the 'web-like' fluid structures, loose forms of belonging and diverse and shifting perspectives as key aspects of contemporary social movements. As Laraña, Johnson and Gusfield (1994: 8) note, new social movements 'in contrast to cadre-led and centralised bureaucracies of political parties' tend to be 'segmented, diffuse and decentralised'. Similarly according to Crook, Pakulski and Waters (1992: 152), new social movements are identified by their 'fuzzy, open, polymorphous and polycephalous' organisation. Writers suggest that this decentralised form of organisation operates as a political statement by movements, in the sense that decentralised movements reject the boundaries and power implications of strict agendas and hierarchical decision making systems (Buechler 2000: 207). Writers claim that these features of NSMs enable these movements to develop multi-level and multi-directional forms of politics that challenge macro and micro-level forms of power in new and creative ways (see Della Porta and Dani 1998; Buechler 2000 for overviews).

Regardless of definitional correctness, the difficulty of categorising forms of identity politics as NSM or as 'political' movements illustrates how debates that surround new social movements in general also apply to profeminism. This chapter suggests that there are sufficient similarities between the forms of politics that profeminism engages in and other contemporary movements to warrant an application of new social movement theory to profeminism.

Connell (2000: 208–10) has developed a different objection to framing profeminism as a social movement. She believes that men's hegemonic position means that they practice a different kind of politics from new social movements. Her main point is that social movements such as feminism and the US civil rights movement formed around the shared exploitation of specific groups. Men, Connell (2000: 209) reminds us, are not an oppressed gendered group and occupy dominant social positions. Therefore Connell (2000: 209–10) argues that there are important differences between men's anti-sexist politics and other social movements that operate around a stigmatised identity.

Moreover, she highlights (2000: 208–10) political reasons why profeminism has to generate a different politics of identity compared with stigmatised groups. She outlines how other identity groups, 'seek the unity of [the] group and assert the dignity of a previously stigmatised identity' (2000: 209). These political objectives for Connell (2000: 209–10) cannot be a part of men's anti-sexist politics because men are privileged and seeking unity focuses profeminist politics on men rather than the groups men oppress.

Connell's observations pinpoint the main disjuncture between profeminism and other left-wing identity movements, and she illustrates why profeminism does not fit neatly into NSM theory. The political recognition of 'despised identities' and the collective reformulations of these identities have been the central markers of left-wing identity movements. Moreover Connell quite rightly indicates the problems that emerge from profeminism emulating new social movement strategies. However seeking the unity of subjugated groups, while an element, is not the only aspect of new social movement politics, and as indicated above, this chapter suggests that analytical mileage can be gained by reading profeminism through NSM frameworks.

The rest of this chapter therefore tries to illustrate the clear similarities that exist between profeminism and NSMs more generally and exposes how profeminism's style of politics raises the same kind of issues about movement strategy that similar styles of political engagement have raised in other movements. A central issue is the relationship between micro and macro forms of power. As the chapters in Part 2 will illustrate, several strands of profeminism try to develop both macro and micro-level forms of political resistance. It also explores the political issues raised by Connell (2000; see also 1993; 1997) and outlined above, in that the chapter outlines the specific questions that arise from the appropriation of identity as a basis for radical politics by a dominant identity. These issues and questions are discussed more fully in Chapter 6.

This exploration of the political style and strategies of profeminism commences with an outline of the differences between older and newer forms of collective political action in post-industrial societies. This chapter then illustrates how profeminist practice mirrors that of newer forms of collective action by identity groups and explores the specific issues these forms of political engagement raise in profeminist politics.

New times, new politics and new men

Touraine (1985) argues that new social movements engage in a different form of politics to earlier working class movements. He argues that new movements such as environmentalism, new age movements and separatist nationalist movements have shifted political protest away from the organisation of labour, economic equality and scarcity to a set of new political issues concerned with people's everyday ways of living, identity and self-image. While debate continues in relation to the characteristics and actual newness of NSM, new social movement theorists argue that the social movements that emerged after the 1960s have been less concerned with relations of production and more concerned with normative frameworks surrounding lifestyle choices and the moral implications of personal practices. (Laraña, Johnson and Gusfield 1994: 6). These movements have been viewed as representing a shift from material politics focused on economic matters towards forms of post-material politics concerned with civil society, culture and identity (see Buechler 2000 for overview).

A range of social changes have been viewed as creating the conditions for new post-material forms of collective political activity to emerge. As the last chapter illustrated, Giddens' (e.g. 1991; 1992; 1999) ideas about the increased introspection around identities in contemporary societies expose several of the economic and cultural factors that have been viewed as generative of identity movements. Another interesting explanation of the emergence of diffuse forms of post-material politics was forwarded by a group of British Marxists in the late 1980s. Using British society and politics as a template, these writers argued that the old class constituencies of left-wing politics found among the male manufacturing class had rescinded and were being replaced by new collective sources of identity and attachment (Hall and Jacques 1989: 451).

These writers claimed that changes in the economy, the effect of globalisation and the politicisation of personal life had moved politics into a new social period, which they termed the 'new times'. Forces of change, according this group of thinkers, had generated new forms of political activism around a plurality of new political concerns and issues, such as gender, race and sexuality; forms of political antagonisms previously sidelined by socialism (Hall and Jacques 1989: 448–53). Theorists of the 'new times,' suggested that taken together these new movements 'move at a similar rhythm' (Hall and Jacques 1989: 36) and challenge culturally and symbolically the positioning of specific identities. Hall (Hall and Jacques 1989: 128) argued that the focus of new identity movements meant that collectively identity movements were engaged in a new democratisation of culture.

As the post-materialist agenda of new social movements shifted the political focus of social movements from the state and political parties towards civil society, culture and the personal, these movements have tended to de-emphasise 'the role of institutions in perpetuating discrimination and exploitation and [highlight] the role of extra-institutional culture' (Kaufman 1990: 71). In contrast older social movements emphasised public institutions as the 'crucial loci of political contestations' (Kaufman 1990: 69).

For Kaufman (1990) this shift in the political orientation of contemporary movements does not only reflect a break with class politics but also represents a general shift by identity movements away from a focus on the state towards concerns about culture and identity. He claims that the movements that organised around racial and women's equality after the Second World War highlighted how inequalities were generated by the state and other social institutions. According to Kaufman, by the 1950s and 1960s the civil rights movement and second wave feminism continued to target the state and institutional sites of power but also expanded the focus of movement activity on to the terrain of cultural representations of identity, self-image and personal politics. For example Kaufman (1990: 70) notes how the American civil rights movement was as much concerned with black Americans' self-image as it was with registering black voters.

Critics of new social movement theory have argued that cultural struggle and identity were always aspects of older movements' activity (see Buechler 2000, Della Porta and Dani 1998; Laraña, Johnson and Gusfield 1994; Tarrow 1994 for overviews). Furthermore movements such as feminism and the LGBM have targeted and challenged the ideologies and practices of social institutions and the activities and policies of the state. However analysts suggest that contemporary identity movements do appear to place much more emphasis on linking the grievances of identity categories to issues of self-definition and autonomy compared with earlier movements (see Melucci 1985; 1989; 1996a). The meaning of identity and the pursuit of counter-hegemonic lifestyles has become a significant element of identity movements, as has the realm of culture, as activists in these movements have increasingly targeted and attacked normative discourses about, for example, race or gender.

Recognising the lifestyle and cultural aspects of identity groups, Habermas (1981: 33–34) has defined the political orientation of contemporary movements as revolving around a concern with the 'grammar of forms of life'. According to Habermas (1981: 33) they are movements fundamentally 'concerned with cultural reproduction, social values and socialisation'. Laraña, Johnson and Gusfield (1994: 7) identify the central characteristics of identity movements as follows: 'they are associated with a set of beliefs, symbols, values and meanings related to sentiments of belonging to a social differentiated group; with the members' image of themselves; and with new, socially constructed attributions about the meaning of everyday life.' The political focus and orientation of contemporary movements mean that they do not fit into the 'dominate image of politics, which is supposed to be pragmatic, technocratic, instrumental, value neutral and increasingly autonomous' (Crook, Pakulski and Waters 1992: 141).

Previously, as Scott (1990, 21) notes, the dominant paradigm of Marxism in the social sciences tended to judge these kinds of pluralist social movements in terms of 'their proximity, or lack of it, to class politics'. In the 'new times' these movements have been viewed by a number of writers as representing new radical forms of political activism, that taken together, expose the new forms of democratic practice organising at the level of civil society in late industrial societies (see especially Laclau and Mouffe 1985).

Other writers have been less sanguine about the orientation and practices of identity movements (Butler 1990; Kaufman 1990). They have raised concerns about the effects of basing politics around identity and also about the political effectiveness of the new movements. Therefore theorists have not only attempted to map social movement antagonisms around power and identity but have engaged in a continuing debate about the potential of these movements to generate new forms of social change and new forms of democracy.

As the above discussion illustrates, new social movement practice is an area of controversy; the later sections of this chapter examine the debates about new social movements as they apply to profeminism. However, before this the next section outlines more clearly the formulation of forms of politics across the categories of identity and power, private and public in profeminism. Concentrating on these issues this section draws out how profeminist practices around the concepts of identity and power exhibit a similar political focus to other forms of gendered and sexual politics.

Gender grievances, men's identities, power and politics

As the previous chapter noted, profeminism has adopted feminist frameworks of gender analysis that illustrate relationships of inequality, injustice and differentials of power between men and women. Therefore contemporary profeminism from its inception organised around a set of grievances about inequity between the sexes, developed by a diverse and plural feminist movement. However, as later chapters illustrate, strands of profeminism tie their gendered politics to different perspectives within feminism to differing degrees. While there are a number of different approaches in profeminism to the feminist movement, overall profeminism recognises and broadly accepts feminist standpoints on gender relationships.

In general profeminism does not only acknowledge that women's identities are sites of power and subjugation, it also connects men's identity at a collective and personal level to feminist grievances and the subjugation of women. Profeminism cultivates and develops the feminist claim that men, while dispersed across different social categories such as race and sexuality, share a collective relationship to the social ideals of manhood, share in the benefits of being the dominant gender and engage individually and as a collective identity in gendered practices that produce and reproduce gender inequities (see for example Hearn 1987a; Hearn and Collinson 1994 and Kimmel 1996; Connell 1995a). It is this formulation of commonality between men that binds together the category of men as a political group in profeminist discourse.

Profeminists have therefore engaged in explorations of the reproduction of gender inequalities through men's behaviour across the diverse constituency of men, and while they accept that gay men and those men positioned in lower social categories do not share in the 'patriarchal dividend' to the same extent, several writers suggest that all men share some kind of either hegemonic or subjugated relationship to the ideals of masculinity (see e.g. Connell 1995).

As Connell (2000: 209–10) notes it is men's social position and the benefits that accrue to them from that position that differentiates profeminism from other forms of identity politics that organise grievances around their own identities rather than those of other groups. However, in terms of its formulation of identity, power and resistance, profeminism operates across a similar cultural and political terrain in relation to other radical forms of gender and sexual politics. Like several expressions of feminist and LGB forms of politics, profeminism takes identity as a 'problematic construct, rather than a natural, taken-for-granted reality' (Messner 1997: 97). Profeminism's problematisation of men's gender identity and gendered relationships operates through NSM formulations of identity politics that operate around cultural struggles, the exploration and re-definition of identity and through examinations of the relationship between macro and micro-levels of power.

Strands of profeminism, to different degrees, acknowledge that public arenas and institutions are involved in the production of gender inequities in terms of institutional policies, practices and organisational structures. For profeminists the social ideals and the individual practices of manhood have institutional supports. For example, by drawing on and extending the feminist analysis of the relationship between social structures, institutions and gender networks of power, profeminists have examined how social policies, the school, the media, the social organisation of the family, sport, leisure and even international global structures produce relationships of inequity between men and women (see e.g. Hoch 1979; Craig 1992; Hearn 1992; Messner and Sabo 1994; Mac an Ghaill 1996; Hearn 1999).

However activists and theorists of profeminism also clearly tie social institutions to the production of men's individual behaviour and identities. Therefore like other gendered and sexual movements, profeminist discourse tends to connect men's personal identities with macro-level institutions and global power structures. Profeminists suggest that the discourses and practices of macro-level structures impact on the behaviour of men at the everyday level. Central to this analysis has been the examination of how institutions and macro-level power structures generate particular ideals of masculinity.

Therefore profeminism interrogates public arenas that produce gender inequalities but also analyses the terrain of everyday life and the interconnections between public and private arenas of power. As Part 2 illustrates, different strands of profeminist thought and politics formulate diverse understandings of these different levels and dimensions of politics. Profeminists have suggested that a range of institutions and social practices produce normative and hegemonic ideals of men's identity. Profeminism therefore struggles on the symbolic field of NSM politics, interrogating the discourses, signs, symbols and images of identity, in this instance manhood, charting these aspects of gender and subjecting them to scrutiny. It also struggles in public arenas to formulate challenges to macro-level forms of power.

The exact ideals of masculinity or manhood, that are valorised by particular societies, as profeminist work exposes, have been difficult to document. Profeminists like Brannon (quoted in Kimmel 1996) have constituted the ideals of masculinity as a particular set of traits: ' ... no sissy stuff ... be a big wheel ... be a sturdy oak ... give 'em hell: exude an aura of manly aggression'. Feminists have produced similar outlines of the typical traits that characterise manhood (see for example Dworkin 1974; Daly 1979). However as Connell (1995) notes, there is no single masculine template. One of the problems with defining the ideals of men's identities is that those ideals are constantly shifting, redefined in different historical periods, different cultures and different contexts. Therefore a stable definition of the ideals of masculinity that men as a collective aspire to and practice is to some extent elusive. Earlier formulations of men's identity tended to adopt a trait approach to defining men's identities; as Part II illustrates, much more sophisticated theories of men's identities have been developed by profeminist writers.

Profeminist explorations of men's identities have developed a number of themes around men's identities that apply to different categories of men to different degrees and vary in relation to men's social and cultural situatedness. The aspects of men's identities that have been most associated with normative masculinity are those practices by certain men that are oppressive to members of other gender communities. Kimmel and Kaufman (1995: 27) outline several of the themes that have become associated with men's identity in profeminism when they write about men's tendency to seek the 'badges of manhood' by engaging in behaviour that is 'emotionally distant, aggressively risk taking, preoccupied with power, status, money, and accumulating sexual partners'. Men's violence, especially men's domestic violence has also become a major theme in strands of profeminism (see e.g. Kaufman 1993; Hearn 1998a).

Expressions of these kinds of behaviour at the micro-level of personal practice and at the macro-level of institutions and the state are therefore viewed by profeminists as thoroughly political and they have attempted to redefine the ideals of masculinity broadly and have also attempted to develop strategies to change men's behaviour, self-definitions and the broader network of power that supports gender inequality (see e.g. Rowan 1987; Hearn 1992; Stoltenberg 2000; Pease 2000). Profeminists therefore, like other NSMs, view the personal level of men's practice as an arena of power and resistance. Several profeminist writers and activists, for example, argue that men exercise power through their reproduction of normative masculinity by, for example, refusing to engage in shared parenting, through violence towards women, and by engaging in behaviour that attempts to dominate and control others. Profeminists suggest that if men engage critically with hegemonic and oppressive male practices then they challenge the exercise of power at the everyday level in their relationships with women, children and other men (see e.g. Rowan 1987; Stoltenberg 2000; Pease 2000). Therefore profeminists incorporate the feminist standpoint that the 'personal is political'. Strands of profeminism also highlight the interconnections between the personal and public levels of power.

The importance of recognising the need to reformulate personal behaviour as part of profeminist politics is also reinforced by the potential hypocrisy of men challenging gender power at the public level and generating gender and sexual inequalities through their everyday practices as men (see Stoltenberg 2000 for comment). While there is disagreement within profeminism on this issue, a significant strand of profeminism suggests that men need to be highly active in challenging and reforming their own behaviour and consciousness. Profeminism develops the idea that masculinity is an arena where men can strive for some degree of self-government in opposition to normative ideals about men's identities, subjectivities and practices, and suggests that changing personal behaviour is an integral part of any men's gender politics (see for e.g. Connell 2000).

The articulation of the possibility of challenging hegemonic forms of gender discourse and practice in profeminist politics is therefore based on an understanding of masculinity as fluid, malleable and changeable. Profeminists view masculinity as socially constituted and open to change at the level of culture and at the level of men's personal self-definitions. Individual identities and lifestyles are identified by profeminists as sites where political changes can occur (see e.g. Rowan 1987; Stoltenberg 2000; Pease 2000).

Profeminism therefore harnesses men's gendered identity politics to feminist visions of changing gender relationships. Some strands of profeminism, discussed in Chapter 8, also emphasise that men's subjectivities are produced in ways that have a negative impact on men. Profeminist writers such as Seidler (e.g. 1997) argue that men are socialised in ways that prevent them from expressing their emotions and establishing positive relationships with other men and children. Seidler (Chapter 8) has been concerned with formulating and exploring grievances against 'the system' of gender relationships and socialisation processes in relation to men. Therapeutic strategies have therefore appeared in profeminist discourses and practices aimed at reforming men's identities and designed to explicate the way that traditional masculinity is insinuated into men's consciousness. Other strands of profeminist thinking, as Part II illustrates, have been more wary of therapeutic practices, preferring more politically engaged forms of politics.

Therefore elements of profeminism exhibit a similar political orientation to other social movements. It deploys its politics across personal identity and stresses 'the shared and thus social nature of individual experience' (Kaufman 1990: 74). Furthermore like other forms of radical gender and sexual politics, profeminism politicises the self within culture and everyday life (Kaufman 1990: 74). It opens up an interrogative space around culture, subjectivity, personal values, norms and agency. Profeminism's stress on refiguring men's identities in counter-hegemonic ways means that profeminism again like other identity movements gives 'political content to choices about lifestyle' (Kaufman 1990: 74). More politically engaged strands also continue to focus on macro-level forms of power and have tried to think through the interconnections between public and private arenas.

NSM orientation is also noticeable in that profeminism is not concerned with gaining power but with tracing forms of power and challenging these forms of power. Furthermore in the profeminist analysis of gender there is no clearly defined centre of power such as the state or clearly defined group responsible for the overall system of gender oppression. This type of understanding of power again reflects the multi-dimensional and fluid agendas of NSM politics more generally. Therefore profeminism, like other identity movements, is inclined towards the goal of increasing democratisation across the whole arena of gender relationships rather than the goals of political control or economic gain (Buechler 2000: 47). The next section examines the complexities that mark this kind of political engagement and style by identity groups.

Profeminism, new social movements and the political

Much of the debate about the impact of NSM politics revolves around how commentators theorise power. If 'real' politics is defined as state orientated and organised around public interventions, agendas and legal campaigns then forms of NSM politics will not be viewed as politically engaged, and aspects of profeminist politics would not be considered as particularly politically effective. In contrast theorists influenced by the work of Foucault suggest that practices that are orientated towards culture and lifestyle changes are thoroughly political as they exploit the indeterminacy of identity and the micro-level of power as arenas of political struggle (see e.g. Lloyd 1996; McLaren 2002).

Foucault formulated a theory of power as productive of subjectivity and socially diffuse (see especially 1980a; 1980b). He (1980a) suggested that power does not repress some intrinsic self that is prior to culture. Instead he tried to illustrate how subjects only become subjects through their production within networks of power. Foucault (1980a) understood power as a complex and diffuse system of discourses and practices spread across society that produce certain ideals of identity that regulate subjects' behaviour and self-definitions. Subjects therefore re-produce power through their behaviour. According to Foucault's analysis there is no inner pre-cultural identity that these regulatory discourses and practices suppress. Rather these discourses actually produce identity (see e.g. 1979; 1980a; 1980b; 1984a; 1984e).

If this analysis is applied to gender identity, gender is theorised as produced through multiple social discourses and does not occur through the direct oppression of a system of centralised power but through everyday ideas, classification, norms and institutional practices and the gendered subjects' own practices (see Lloyd 1993; 1996). For Foucault subjectivity and the arena of everyday life are saturated by power.

Foucault's radical conceptualisation of power opens up an analysis of the operation of power beyond the narrowly defined political realm of economics, political institutions and the state, and identifies the micro-level of society and personal identity as sites of political contestation (see Ashe 1999). Foucault's (1980a) 'analytics' of power therefore suggests that movements' struggles around everyday experiences, practices and definitions of identity are thoroughly political and engaged in subverting the myriad examples of social power that operate at the micro-level of society (see Buechler 2000).

While Foucault's non-normative stance and deconstruction of key political categories have troubled some feminists, several have found Foucault's focus on the micro-political level of power helpful for opening up new and diverse modes of resistance against the multiple forms of power that make up gender relationships of power (Fraser 1989a; 1989b; 1989c; Lloyd 1993; 1996). As suggested above, profeminism operates in this arena. Operating at the micro-level, profeminists have followed the feminist strategy of opening new spaces to articulate counter-hegemonic identities and knowledges around the category of men. Certain strands, like certain schools of feminism, have also been heavily focused on macro-level forms of power but, as specific chapters in Part II illustrate, not to the exclusion of issues concerning identity and the micro-level of power.

Melucci works on a different theoretical terrain to Foucault. However, Melucci (1989) also suggests that identity groups, 'announce' that something else is possible in relation to identities. Melucci (1985: 801–13) argues that the emergence of an identity movement is therefore in itself a political success. This is because the emergence of a movement suggests that an alternative to current social practices and norms is available. In this respect, the establishment of a movement is in itself 'a symbolic challenge to the dominant patterns [of society]' (Melucci 1985: 801).

If we apply Foucault's and Melucci's ideas about the possibility of challenging what might be called social power through making problematic or refusing normative identities, then profeminism can certainly be viewed as politicising men's identity, opening the category up to political scrutiny thereby locating it fully in the political arena. Therefore profeminism can be viewed broadly as set of political practices that refuse or reject the closure of the traditional boundaries of men's identities and explores the constitution of those identities through attention to micro-level and macro-level forces and relationships.

Profeminism's orientation to the NSM practices of scrutinising identity and everyday life means that its political activity also subverts the categories of private/public. The deconstruction of traditional formulations of the political as encompassing the public sphere only has been fiercely attacked by feminists (see e.g. Pateman 1988). Feminists argue that many of the processes involved in women's subjugation occur across the private realm and in interpersonal relationships. Defining this arena as private rather than political means that aspects of gender power are sidelined from the analysis of power and politics. Profeminism also targets traditional definitions of what is political and what is private, pre-contractual and natural through its focus on the politics of men's everyday lives. This is not limited to profeminism's continuation of the feminist movement's strategy of disputing the naturalness of men's gender identity and re-defining it as political, but can also be seen in the specific effects of profeminist strategies on traditional understandings of the private/public divide. In this respect profeminism, like feminism challenges finer forms of power and not just state or macro-institutional forms of power.

For example profeminism's focus on identities means that like other identity movements it breaks down the barrier between everyday life and political participation thereby disrupting the private/public divide (Buechler 2000: 207). This is because personal action and public institutions and structures become conceptually fused in this form of politics (Laraña, Johnston and Gusfield 1994: 7).

The impact of profeminism's NSM focus on the disruption of the public/private divide can be seen in another example directly related to its political practices. A common aspect of some forms of profeminism has been what might be called a tendency towards 'confessional' discourses. This involves men articulating and developing narratives of their personal lives and feelings as men. Nedelmann (1984: 1035) notes that: 'Underlying the cult of making confessions in public is a change in the social definition of what belongs to the private sphere and therefore should be private, and what belongs to the political sphere and should be made public'. This strategy is seemingly especially disruptive in profeminist practice as emotional discourses are being articulated by men who, according to the discourses of normative masculinity, do not engage in this emotional story telling. In practice these strategies are more complex but this example illustrates the terrain of profeminist antagonisms (see Chapter 7).

For Laclau and Mouffe (1985) NSMs that operate through these kinds of contestations are thoroughly engaged politically. Laclau and Mouffe argue that movements operating outside formal political structures that insist on the importance of the personal, moral and affective aspects of life are expressions of a radical democratic impulse that has developed in late capitalism. Movements that challenge hegemonic relationships around gender, sexuality, peace and the environment are democratic in two senses for Laclau and Mouffe.

Laclau and Mouffe suggest that NSMs, unlike class politics, do not universalise struggle by reducing it to a single determinant. Rather they engage with particular forms of power and in this sense they are particularistic struggles against certain forms of subjugation across identity or environmental concerns. However, according to Laclau and Mouffe they also have a universal element in that they attempt to extend democratic discourse within liberal democracy by struggling around the definition of 'floating signifiers' such as equality and liberty. These movements also call for a 'multiplication of spaces' within liberal democracy where relationships traditionally viewed as non-political, like gender, are reconfigured as antagonistic and illegitimate. Under the terms of Laclau and Mouffe's theory profeminism operates within a broader arena of radical democratic politics and struggles around the cultural and political antagonisms of gender and sexuality.

Critics of contemporary movements however question the NSM orientation towards politics and their oppositional practices. Kaufman (1990), for example, has argued that contemporary identity politics are marked by the practices of 'anti-politics'. Kaufman suggests that contemporary identity movements have emphasised personal, identity and lifestyle to the point where these movements' politics have become apolitical, largely introspective and orientated around insulated therapeutic practices.

For Kaufman identity politics' stress on the private, personal aspects of lifestyle has meant that the public sphere tradition of social movements has weakened (Kaufman 1990: 79). He argues that 'the tendency to claim political content for changes in lifestyle encourages the view that politics need not necessarily involve engagement with external structures of power' (Kaufman 1990: 77). Kruks (2001: 88) echoes this point when she suggests that the earlier politics of recognition led to the formulation of clear political demands by identity groups: 'By contrast, in [contemporary] identity politics demands of respect and recognition often remain on a psychological and experiential plane and do not translate into programs for legal or institutional change'. Furthermore Kaufman claims (1990: 75) that identity politics in some respects reflects the dominant cultural patterns of individualisation in that these movements' emphasis on lifestyle and individual choices mirrors the ideology of the capitalist marketplace.

Kruks (1988: 2001) reflects these concerns when she suggests that 'appearance frequently becomes central to identity politics: how one dresses, what badges one wears, how one's hair is styled become more important, as do what one reads, what music one listens to, what one eats and where one "hangs out"'.

Strands of profeminism, as Part II illustrates, have been marked by the kind of therapeutic strategies that Kaufman identifies in other contemporary movements. The effects of therapeutic strategies however, as subsequent chapters will illustrate, are not predetermined or clear cut. However, Kaufman does flag up important concerns about the relationship between personal styles of politics and the effectiveness of movements to engender wider political changes. Furthermore his critique of NSMs suggests that careful study of movement discourse and strategy is required to understand the dynamics of personal and micro-level politics.

Other theorists have had concerns about the deployment of the category of identity itself in social movements. Butler (1990) has interrogated the effects of organising around identity in the women's movement and has raised a number of concerns about the effects of deploying gender identity as a foundation for radical movements. Butler (1990), unlike Kaufman, has little to say about the public level of movement activity and instead concentrates on the exclusionary, universalising and essentialist impact of taking identity as a unitary category for resistance. For Butler all identities are multiple and blended, produced through diverse identifications and modalities of power. Identity politics, she claims, universalises the concerns and experiences of some aspects of identities over others; therefore identity claims can produce exclusions within movements. This issue of exclusion was manifest in the feminist movement, as the perspectives of white, middle class feminists tended to sideline the standpoints of women of colour and working class women (Butler 1990).

Furthermore, Butler (1990) claims that by instantiating identity as a foundation for political resistance, political movements may be reproducing the very power they which to subvert. This concern arises, she claims, because this kind of politics reinforces cultural categorisations of specific groups, as having certain differences from other groups which are socially constituted myths of identity that tie people to certain social ideals of identity, usually produced through normative modalities of power. Following Foucault, Butler views subjectivity and the norms of identity as contingent, cultural forces which are reinforced through their appropriation as a foundation for political claims and resistance by identity groups. Butler (1990) therefore argues for forms of political resistance that 'displace' identities through practices that disrupt the stability of identity categories.

Foucault makes a similar observation when he suggested that by invoking identity as a basis for politics, groups remain within the logic of the technologies of power that produces those identities (1980b). Foucault's (see especially 1980a; 1980b) work suggests a genealogical approach to identity that exposes identity as an effect of a complex network of power relations, produced through complex discursive struggles, and he has acknowledged the disruptive aspects of identity movements that refuse identity (Foucault 1982). Therefore Butler suggests that radical strategies will work towards configuring gender and sexuality as critical sites of deconstruction, thereby refusing the tendency towards basing movements on the fiction of the homogeneous experiences of groups.

Bulter's and Kaufman's analysis also highlights the problem of creating coalitions with other groups. The tendency of some forms of identity politics to turn towards introspective forms of therapeutic practices means that it is difficult to build effective political alliances with other political movements that may share similar concerns about the relationship between identities and power or who may have cross-cutting identities. Furthermore the problem of experiential exclusivity that Butler's work highlights may again make it difficult to develop coalitions around forms of power. As Kruks observes:

> the argument is generally made that outsiders have no basis from which they can legitimately evaluate the group's claims about its knowledge, or those political or moral positions that it takes on the basis of them. In short, only those who live a particular reality can know about it, and only they have the right to speak.
> (2001: 109)

Other feminists have complained that gendered politics should not be about identity but about securing justice though legal, institutional and state orientated strategies (see McLaren 2002: 120 for discussion). However, as will be discussed in more detail in subsequent chapters, political identity and political agendas are often linked in complex ways. For example the identities, experiences and standpoints of groups affected by power can influence their articulation of agendas for justice. Overall then the practices of contemporary identity politics raise a range of political concerns. As profeminism, partly, operates on this terrain of politics, these concerns are important in any analysis of the profeminist strategies. While the micro-arena of gender relations represents a field of power relationships that can be challenged by micro-level political antagonisms, the exercise of oppositional agency within this arena is complex and may produce its own set of power effects.

However other concerns about profeminism's deployment of NSM strategies emerge from its instantiation of men's identities as a point for feminist politics. The contentions that surround identity politics are amplified by profeminism's appropriation of a dominant identity as a basis for radical oppositional politics. The next section outlines these issues which subsequent chapters 'flesh' out.

Men, feminism and identity

As the above discussion illustrated, feminists have been at the forefront of developing new social movement styles of politics. However a number of feminists have been concerned about the appropriation of men's identity as a basis for feminist politics. As indicated in Chapter 1, certain feminist commentators have argued that some men are reproducing existing relationships of power through their gendered politics. Critics of profeminism have suggested that particular men may exploit feminism to their own advantage, for example, by using profeminism as a means to gain research funding, to 'take over' and to sideline women's perspectives (Canaan and Griffin 1990; Spark 1994).

Furthermore some feminists, focusing on certain strands of profeminism, have claimed that the 'cultural laboratory' of therapeutic practice has led to an introspective politics of 'me tooism' as men explore how the ideals of masculinity affect them as men. A number of feminists have argued that these practices have little connection to changing gender relationships more broadly and may be detrimental to women (Hester 1984; Babcock and McKay 1995; Rapping 1996;). Therefore, for example, while the confessional, discussed earlier, may disrupt the public/private divide it may also produce other gendered effects in the form of discourses about men's pain and men's needs, sidestepping the important relationship between men's subjectivities and power. Therefore issues have emerged around the inscription of men's 'pain' into profeminist politics.

Another problem has arisen around the issue of experiential exclusivity. Question marks hang over men's ability to produce feminist standpoints and knowledges from the position of the oppressor. 'In the extreme, this suggests that knowledge arises from an experiential basis that is so profoundly group specific that others, who are outside of the group and who lack its immediate experiences, cannot share that knowledge' (Kruks 2001: 109). And the conclusions that some feminists draw from this claim is that 'those who do not experience domestic violence, or incest, or rape, or unwanted pregnancy, or even unequal pay have no experiential basis from which to evaluate, and no right to speak about such issues' (Kruks 2001: 111).

Furthermore several feminists have queried whether subjects, who benefit from gender relationships can really be fully committed to feminist ideals, which raises the concern that men may simply be acting as 'tourists' in relation to feminist scholarship and politics (Moore 1998). These concerns have meant that the issue of coalition building across gendered communities is marked by a range of concerns about the possibilities and effects of profeminist politics.

Therefore in contrast to Melucci's claim that the establishment of a movement is itself a challenge to power, feminist critics of profeminism suggest that aspects of men's feminism may actually support and reproduce existing patterns of power. While profeminism may be operating in the arena of NSM politics and may be deploying contemporary identity movement strategies, when it comes to the analysis of this form of politics 'the devil may be in the detail' of specific profeminist practices and discourses.

Chapter 6 evaluates feminist critiques of profeminism in more detail and continues to develop an analytical framework for the examination of different prominent profeminist writers who have tried to develop frameworks for profeminist politics in Chapters 6 to 10. McCarthy and Zald (1973) point out that leadership is important in NSMs. McCarthy and Zald argue that leaders define the movement's ideology and agenda. Dominant voices have emerged within profeminism that have struggled to forge different forms of politics depending on their position in relation to the internal dynamics of the movement and the influence of external discourses by other gendered groups. These writers expose the differences between strands of profeminism and articulate the central strategies of the movement. These frameworks highlight the kind of internal debates that have emerged within profeminism about the issues that surround men's feminist identity politics and identity movement strategies more generally.

However profeminist discourse and practice has also been defined in relation to the agendas and discourses of other gender-conscious men's groups and movements. The next chapter therefore explores these groups and highlights the similarities and differences between these groups and profeminist politics. It also details other men's groups' perceptions of the profeminist movement and why these groups have opposed profeminism's agenda.

5 The Politics of Non-feminist Men's Groups

The field of men's gender politics

> In passing, also, I would like to say that the first time Adam had a chance he laid the blame on woman.
>
> Nancy Astor (1993: 44)

As highlighted earlier, the politics that surrounded masculinities from the 1960s has been pluralistic. A number of alternative gender-conscious men's groups have emerged alongside the profeminist movement and have developed discourses and agendas around men's identities in relation to contemporary gender relationships. These groups have developed a range of divergent discourses around themes such as men's identities, the crisis of masculinity and gender power. Collectively, alternative groups' interpretations of these categories challenge profeminist accounts of gender subjectivity and inequality. As subsequent chapters will illustrate, profeminists often define their politics in relation to the discourses developed by these men. Some strands of profeminism completely reject the perspectives of alternative gender-conscious men's groups.

Other strands have argued that profeminism needs to 'listen' to some of the issues about modern masculinity that have been raised by other men who have been exploring their identities outside of the boundaries of feminist standpoints. This chapter discusses the discourses and agendas of three forms of men's gender-conscious politics and exposes the differences between these groups and profeminism generally (Clatterbaugh 1990; Messner 1997). This chapter focuses on specific examples of groups that have emerged in US and UK contexts (see Hearn and Hertta 2006; Hearn and Holmgren 2006 for analysis of the Scandinavian context).

Conservative men's groups

There are a number of conservative men's groups, including religious groups and men's rights groups (see Hearn and Hertta 2006). One of the main characteristics of these groups is that they want to conserve traditional gender relationships. A number of conservative men's groups developed out of the men's rights movement. These groups formed in opposition to changes in family law arising from an increase in divorce. In the wake of divorce many men found that their control over their families was weakened. Groups concerned with men's rights began organising in opposition to divorce reform and custody issues around the 1960s. One of the earliest documented American men's rights group is the conservative Divorce Reform Busters founded by Rubin Kidd and George Partis in 1960. The men involved in this early organisation believed that family and divorce law discriminated against them and favoured their wives (see MDA 2000).

Originally men's rights groups had a narrow focus. Groups such as the Divorce Reform Busters were mainly interested in legal matters pertaining to divorce and custody. However in the 1970s some men's rights groups broadened their agenda beyond legal rights and constructed discourses on a variety of issues pertaining to gender relationships. These men believed that it was not only men's rights in the family that were being questioned against the political background of feminism. They also believed that the legitimacy of their traditional gender identity was coming under attack. By the mid-1970s most of these groups had incorporated claims about biological differences between the sexes into their discourses.

Charles V. Metz was a key figure in broadening the focus of conservative men's groups to include a theory of male and female subjectivity. Metz's (1968) pamphlet *Divorce and Custody for Fathers* claimed that men and women have natural social roles which had been subverted due to the influence of feminism. Feminists, according to Metz, had induced gullible men to construct laws against the interests of their own gender. Metz argued that society needed to return to traditional gender roles and that men needed to re-instate themselves as head of the household. Metz's pamphlet provided a broader framework for conservative men's groups. His ideas about the naturalness of male power in both the public and private sphere and his claim that feminists were responsible for the erosion of 'male' rights continue to underpin the discourse of certain conservative men's groups.

Richard Doyle, a member of the American Society of Divorced Men, expanded Metz's more general approach. In 1976 Doyle wrote the *Rape of the Male*. This text elaborates Metz's claim that society needs to return to traditional and natural gender roles. Doyle also developed Metz's idea that modern men have been victimised by feminism and subjected to unfair social practices. Doyle formed his own men's group in 1975 called the Men's Rights Association, which he later renamed the Men's Defence Association (MDA). This organisation is still active and represents conservative men's discourse on masculinity (see MDA 2000).

Such groups also operate in the UK. The UK's main conservative group is the United Kingdom Men's Movement, formerly the Cheltenham Group. Like the MDA, the UKMM developed out of issues pertaining to divorce and maintenance payments. As the group developed, it broadened its agenda to provide 'a coherent intellectual base' to the fathers' rights movement and anti-feminist men generally (UKMM 1995: 3). The UKMM campaign for men's rights rests on a discourse similar to that of the MDA.

Gilder's (1973; 1986) writings on modern gender relationships also provided many of the ideas about men's identities and gender relationships employed by conservative men's groups. Like Metz and Doyle, Gilder makes the claim that gender subjectivity is determined by biological factors. Gilder argues that masculinity is naturally violent and destructive. He claims that men are biologically predisposed by nature to seek instant gratification through whatever means is available to them. While for Gilder this bestial subjectivity represents the 'true' nature of men's identity, he also maintains that men's natural subjectivity does not necessarily determine the kind of subjects that men are capable of becoming. Gilder claims that certain social arrangements can direct men's natural propensity to violence and aggression into socially productive behaviour. If society is organised along patriarchal lines and socialises men into the protector/provider role, then male aggression, according to Gilder, will be channelled into work and the pursuit of a career.

Gilder believes that the family is a key institution for socialising men into socially productive roles. The family, he claims, harnesses men's energies into caring for their dependants, thereby suppressing the male propensity towards destructive behaviour. Also marriage ensures that men's allegedly uncontrollable sexuality is contained within a monogamous relationship.

For Gilder the protector/provider role represents the best identity that men can assume given their potentially bestial subjectivity. Gilder constructs traditional masculinity as representing the only socially viable authentic identity for men. The protector/provider role, Gilder maintains, is the only social role that will ensure that men become productive members of society. If society fails to provide this role for men they will revert back to a naturally violent masculinity, or will turn to drugs, violence or alcoholism.

Clearly women have a key role to play in the socialisation or civilisation of men in this construction of normative masculinity. Gilder contends that if men are to be civilised women must assume their traditional gender identity and use their erotic power to harness men's behaviour into the protector/provider role. Indeed, for Gilder, women need to strike a sort of bargain with men, the woman must agree to give the man sexual pleasure in return for monogamy and marriage. In this kind of relationship, Gilder claims, women can assume the role of nurturer and exercise their natural capacities by caring for the family and home. Gilder's analysis of men's identity suggests that neither patriarchy nor traditional masculinity is natural; instead they are social 'contrivances,' effects of socialisation processes that 'tame' natural masculinity and direct it into functional social roles. However patriarchy is legitimated by the claim that this kind of social organisation is good for society and enables men and women to assume functional roles.

Therefore for conservatives, feminists have undermined functional gender roles eroding the institutional supports of patriarchy and have attacked men and masculinity. Conservative writers claim that in modern society feminism has created a situation that has led to men losing their traditional dominance in the workplace and the home. According to conservatives, as the pathology of feminism has spread through society, men's traditional rights have been taken away from them – they have become victims of feminist attack. Contemporary men, they argue, are thrown out of their homes by women, refused custody of their children by the courts, and forced to pay maintenance to women and children that they no longer live with (UKMM 1995: 13). In the workplace men are losing their jobs because 'mediocre women' are being promoted at the expense of able men (UKMM 1995: 3).

Employers, they claim, are pushing men further out of the workplace by providing day-care facilities for employees' children and by holding jobs for pregnant women. Men also live in fear of being falsely accused of sexual harassment (UKMM 1995: 9). Richard Doyle asserts that the 'male of the species is under increasing attack legally, politically, economically, and culturally'. Contemporary men, he tells us, are caught 'in a deadly web' of 'discrimination and misandry' (Doyle 1999).

For conservatives the current malaise of masculinity is therefore attributed to women and feminist women in particular. Bauroth

(2000), a contributor to the conservative *Liberator* magazine claims that contemporary 'woman drinks, gambles, curses, hits and in between sambas, flushes her new-born down the toilet'. It is the age of 'Neanderthal' woman. Recent tampering with traditional gender roles, conservatives claim, has produced an increase in violence, teenage pregnancy, killer kids, a feminised, weak army and a corrupt government.

Conservative groups argue that feminism has not only destroyed the institutional supports of masculinity and male rights, it has also denigrated manhood. Modern feminism seeks to establish a lesbian feminist republic and reduce men's role in society until they become socially redundant. The MDA claim that currently 'covens of feminoids' are conspiring against men, under the cover of women's shelters, aided and abetted 'by their camp followers' (Doyle 1999). The 'feminazis', they claim, have turned women against men and have run an anti-male campaign with the help of politicians and the judiciary. The feminist onslaught on the 'male gender' has 'left men like animals caught in car headlights' (Doyle 1999).

The UKMM and the MDA campaign for the re-establishment of male rights and male power in a number of social arenas. These two groups respectively demand a repeal of the Sex Discrimination Act in the UK and the Equal Rights Amendments in the US. Furthermore these groups argue for the suppression of equal opportunities legislation and bodies. Both seek the removal of obligations placed on employers to hold jobs for pregnant women and argue for an end to tax breaks for child care facilities in the workplace. Both groups also demand an end to paternity leave in institutions where it has been established. These two conservatives groups claim that these changes must be accompanied by changes in family law. Each group campaigns for legal changes that will ensure that no spouse can remove the other spouse or children from the marital home. In order to re-establish men's roles as fathers they seek a removal of all welfare incentives to single mothers (www.md.org; UKMM 1995).

In addition to this, both groups call for a re-establishment of male control over and access to women's bodies. For example, the UKMM want marital sex to be excluded from the definition of rape or any other criminal offence. Both groups argue that sexual harassment laws should be removed and each demands that husbands have the right to consultation on matters such as abortion, contraception and sterilisation. Clearly this is a defensive agenda that seeks to re-establish the institutional supports of men's power (UKMM 1995).

This kind of 'male' victimisation and rights discourse also emerges in some fathers' rights groups. For example, fathers' rights groups represent women as 'mendacious and vindictive mothers' and claim victim status in relation to custody and alimony issues (Kaye and Tolmie 1998). Other conservative groups such as the Promise Keepers develop a less antagonistic discourse around women. The Promise Keepers is a faith-based Christian movement that stresses men's failure to act as 'servants' and 'leaders' in their families and encourages men to be more involved fathers and husbands (see Heath 2004; Messner 1997). However this group also constitutes men and women's identities as biologically and spiritually determined.

Conservative groups have therefore responded to social changes in men's identities through the deployment of very traditional discourses about men and women's identities. Conservative claims about the nature of gender identity have been operative in the production of matrices of gender oppression for centuries. It is hardly surprising that some men, concerned about the erosion of stable conceptions of manhood and men's power, should be attracted to this kind of discourse as it harks back to a 'golden age' of patriarchy. Furthermore the claim that gender is a product of biology facilitates the constitution of a fixed and natural conception of manhood that some heterosexual men can identify with, amid the contemporary shifting of their identity. This biological discourse also operates to create fictions of identity that give the illusion that masculinity may be fixed in ways that stabilise the ontological disruptions around men's identities in late capitalist societies. Therefore in contrast to profeminism which seeks to explore the malleability of men's identities these men try to fix men in an ahistorical, pre-cultural, biological identity.

Profeminism has been concerned to explore how differences between men break down relatively settled and fixed definitions of men's identity. The conservative groups examined in this section by contrast, try to generate the notion that differences among men are not a manifestation of the possibilities for different forms of manhood. Some men's groups construct the idea that non-normative masculinities, such as gay masculinities, are distorted variations of a 'true' or original, biological masculinity. Gay men come under frequent attack from groups such as the MDA.

However Heath (2003) argues that there are some aspects of conservative discourses on men's identities that may be disruptive. For example, she (Heath 2003: 441) argues that the Promise Keepers' emphasis on men discussing their responsibilities to their families and other men means that they 'embrace an expressive masculinity that is frowned on by the dominant culture'.

Similarly other aspects of conservative engagements with masculinity disrupt traditional discourses about gender as this discourse becomes tailored to contemporary conditions. For example in response to the feminist exposure of men's violence towards women, some conservative writers have claimed that women are more violent than men. Moreover, in order to support claims for custody, conservatives have suggested that men can bring up children as well as, if not better than, women. The MDA paints a picture of lone fathers as emotionally warm, loving and capable parents. The problem for conservative men in relation to these claims is that if men, as they contend, need traditional patriarchal roles to quell their violent nature, how could a man reform his masculinity as a lone father outside of the boundaries of traditional marriage so successfully?

Conservatives have also undermined their own discourse of female domesticity in their eagerness to expose what they believe to be the inadequacy of women. According to their research, 80% of women regularly fail to find a clean cup because they use all their cups before they will wash one, casting doubt on women's natural domesticity (MDA 2000). Even if this were true, it could be noted that washing several cups together is more economical. Regardless, these attacks on women illustrate that in the 'new times' men do not only employ old patriarchal ideas about essentialist gender identities. In the context of feminism, these men have also attacked women's capabilities as mothers and carers in order to legitimise their custody claims and have built up some associations between masculinity, childcare and nurturing. In their attempt to secure traditional rights for men over women in the conditions of late capitalism these men have been forced into developing new visions of fatherhood, albeit underpinned by highly anti-feminist discourses and agendas. Of course groups like the MDA also seek to undermine legal protections against domestic violence, and one of the effects of their agenda would be that violent men could gain easier access to women and children.

This kind of formulation of contemporary masculinity has not drawn many active supporters. More men have been drawn to mythopoetic discourses discussed below. However writers such as Charles Murray (1995) have deployed similar ideas to frame debates on poverty and crime in American and British cities. Murray claimed that the trend toward single parenthood among young women in both countries has left young men without the civilising influence of marriage. Murray claims that the breakdown of the traditional family structure in poor communities has created a new underclass of work-shy and aggressive males (see Messner 1997). Other groups shift from more traditional essentialist accounts of masculinity. These groups have developed discourses of men's liberation. Liberationist discourses emerged in profeminism and anti-feminist discourses around masculinity. The next section examines anti-feminist liberationist groups.

Liberationists

There are a number of affinities between the liberationist and conservative discourses on masculinity (see Clatterbaugh 1992). Elements of liberationist discourse also emerge in some forms of profeminism (see Chapter 8). However, certain groups of men have developed a discourse around masculinity that concentrates on exposing the negative effects of men's roles, rejects feminism and seeks to preserve men's traditional rights. Such groups have, to some extent, emerged through the fathers' rights movement but, unlike conservative groups, liberationists have been more influenced by theories that view masculinity as socially constituted rather than biologically determined. Most anti-feminist liberationists argue that traditional masculinity is not the manifestation of an intrinsic 'male' identity but is imposed on men by society. Liberationist groups, such as the one discussed below, present themselves as being involved in an attack on society's ideal of manhood. Men who are members of this kind of group claim that the traditional male role has oppressed and psychologically damaged men. Liberationist groups such as the National Coalition of Free Men (NCFM) state that their aim is to develop a new identity for men beyond traditional definitions that will free them from enslavement to normative forms of masculinity.

Therefore liberationists view themselves as being involved in a critical examination of traditional 'male identity' (see Baumli 1985). The NCFM is one of the longest established anti-feminist liberationist groups in the US. The NCFM developed out of Free Men Inc., a fathers' rights group formed in Columbia, Maryland, in 1977. Between 1977 and 1980 new chapters of Free Men were formed in other parts of US. During the 1980s the chapters joined to form the National Coalition which operates with a men's rights agenda. Liberationist discourse has its origins in versions of both profeminism and men's rights discourse.

The framework for liberationist discourse on male identity can be traced to the 1970s. The intellectual base of the liberationist agenda is much more modern than that of the conservative groups. Feminist analysis of women's social roles in the 1960s and 1970s opened up a framework for men to explore their social roles. Writings by men on their identity began to appear in the 1970s. During this period a number of publications by men dealt critically with men's social role. Sex role theory provided the discursive underpinning for much of men's early writing on the subject of their gender identity. The liberationists entered into an exploration of the constitution of masculinity and its effect on men's lives and roles. Academic books such as Brannon and David's (1975) *The 49% Majority*, Fasteau's (1974) *The Male Machine* and Pleck's (1981) *The Myth of Masculinity* argued that the 'male role' had negative consequences for men and should be reconstituted in ways that would liberate both men and women. These books operated to open a conceptual framework, sympathetic to feminism, through which the negative aspects of the 'male role' could be explored. Several of the early liberationists explored masculinity with reference to feminist theories of male power (see Clatterbaugh 1990).

The two key intellectual sources of the NCFM, Warren Farrell and Herb Goldberg, entered into this kind of examination of masculinity during this period (see NCFM 2007a). In 1975 Farrell wrote *The Liberated Male*. In this book Farrell explores the negative effects of masculinity, while accepting the feminist analysis of men as a 'dominant gender.' Farrell had a close relationship with feminism during the writing of the *Liberated Man*. He worked alongside the National Coalition of Women and was involved in organising men's support groups. Goldberg's relationship to feminism in the 1970s was more precarious, although he was not openly hostile to it (Clatterbaugh 1990).

In the late 1970s and early 1980s Farrell and Goldberg's view of feminism and masculinity changed. They rejected the feminist claim that men monopolise power and use it to oppress women. These two writers constructed the idea that men have little power over their identity and claimed that men were as much the victims of socially constructed gender roles as women. Farrell and Goldberg apply this kind of analysis to the male role and claim that men are also oppressed by the role society imposes on them. What the liberationists refuse is feminism's claim that male identity enables men to attain power over women in society.

In 1993 Farrell published *The Myth of Male Power*. The book is a direct attack on the feminist analysis of gender-based power. In this book Farrell criticised the feminist claim that men hold and exercise power over women. Farrell, while seemingly keen to question established 'male identity', reformulated the feminist understanding of masculinity and power. He argued that men are the oppressed gender not women.

Herb Goldberg (1976) offered a similar analysis. He accused feminism of berating men when men are the true victims of the social construction of gender identity. These claims underpin much of the current anti-feminist liberationist discourse on masculinity. In an attempt to construct the idea that masculinity is a culturally oppressed subject position, not a position of power, Farrell and Goldberg claim that the negative traits that are associated with traditional masculinity, such as violence, aggressiveness and assertiveness are not natural manifestations of a masculine identity. These traits, according to Farrell (1993) and Goldberg (1976), are a response by men to the burdens of the 'male role'. They are not strategies men use to oppress women, as feminists would have it. Farrell and Goldberg both claim that men are socialised into a male identity that they have to live up to if they are to be accepted as real men. Living up to these socially constructed ideals, they claim, places a great deal of strain on the men. Goldberg states that:

> Traditional masculinity is largely a psychologically defensive operation. A man's psychological energy is used to defend against proving to himself and others what he is not; feminine, dependent, emotionally passive, afraid, helpless, a loser, a failure, impotent and so on.
>
> (1976: 6)

Furthermore the male role is contradictory. According to the liberationists, masculine identity has always created a crisis for men. They argue that society has set up contradictory ideals for men. Hayward (1987: 12) writes that men:

> are told to be gentle, while gentle men are told they are wimps. Men are told to be vulnerable, but vulnerable [men] are told that they are too needy. Men are told to be less performance orientated, but less successful men are rejected for their lack of ambition. The list of contradictions is seemingly endless.
>
> (1987: 12)

Men, Farrell (e.g. 1993) maintains, respond to the difficulties of men's identity in negative ways. They can despair, become violent or, in the worst case scenario, kill themselves. Farrell and Goldberg are both keen to construct masculinity as a victim identity. They compile a catalogue of the costs of being a man in modern society. Farrell (1993) argues that the male sex role is the reason for men's higher mortality rate – men die 10 years earlier than women. Farrell argues that this amounts to a '10% male disposability tax' being placed on men because of their role. Farrell finds further evidence of the negative effects of the male role (1993: 115) in men's suicide rates. Adolescent men commit suicide at four times the rate of adolescent women he claims. Men, he asserts, also suffer more from addiction and other destructive behaviour. For Farrell male addiction is not, as the conservatives would claim, a product of the failure to attain a traditional masculine subject position but is a consequence of trying to achieve it.

For liberationists men have to try to deal with these problems but liberationists' claim men's socialisation means that they have very few emotional resources to draw on. Men are in crisis, Farrell (1993: 18–24) asserts because they do not have the power to define their own identity. They are pushed into traditional models of manhood and suffer the burdens of the male role. The NCFM constructs a discourse of masculinity on the basis of this kind of analysis.

The NCFM (2007) states that one of its key objectives is to attack the idea that 'men have all the power' and that 'women are a special oppressed group'. The NCFM, in line with the ideas of Goldberg and Farrell, claims that men's negative behaviour is not something that is intrinsic to men but is a product of the social organisation of gender and the demands that society makes on them.

Feminism, liberationists argue, has not addressed the problems that the male gender role creates for men. These men maintain that feminism is only interested in running a hate campaign against men. Instead of attempting to create equality between the sexes, feminism has attempted to eradicate the male role altogether, particularly men's roles as fathers. Along with eradicating the male role, feminists, the liberationists argue, have demonised men in order to strip them of their rights. Men, they claim, have been victimised by an unfair legal system, have been deprived of access to children and burdened with providing financial support to women and children just because they are men. The creation of equal opportunities in the workplace, according to the liberationists, has deprived men of jobs. Therefore, men have been asked to keep their traditional roles but have been deprived of the means to achieve them (see Clatterbaugh 1990: 87). Liberationists maintain 'male' bashing and victimisation have increased male guilt and men's feelings of failure and inadequacy. According to Farrell (1993), feminists have been able to disempower men by cultivating the notion that men have a monopoly on social and economic power. Farrell claims that the idea of male power is a feminist fallacy. For Farrell men take jobs and earn money that women spend.

In the current conditions, according to the NCFM (2007), many men 'are no longer comfortable with the traditional "male roles". Emotionally adrift, they are searching for a new identity; yet they find few viable alternatives to traditional masculine behavior'. The NCFM (2007) states that the 'change and flux of these times seem to provide an excellent opportunity to redefine options for men in ways which will allow them to develop according to their needs, desires and potentials'.

Liberationists seem intent on challenging the conservatives' construction of an intrinsic male identity. The conservatives argue that men's destructive biological propensity means that the only positive identity that is open to them is the protector/provider role. Liberationist discourse seems to challenge this traditional 'truth' of men's identity. In other words, the anti-feminist liberationists seem to be involved in a problematisation of traditional masculinity and the discourses that have been involved in its production; of course they do this through an anti-feminist discourse.

For example, the NCFM refuse the idea that men are innately destructive and violent. This organisation also supports programmes designed to 'free' men from violent and destructive behaviour, something they believe to be produced through men's socialisation as opposed to their biology. The anti-liberationists also suggest that they are involved in an unhinging of the notion that men are biologically suited to the protector/provider role. Therefore liberationists seem to have some kind of similarity with profeminism in that these groups see masculinity as malleable and seek to re-invent men's identities in new non-traditional ways. The liberationists are also concerned with recognising the effect that normative 'male' identities have on gay men and other men who refuse to conform to this model.

However on closer inspection liberationists do not shift men's identities very far from traditional models of manhood. The liberationists claim that their mission is to 'free' men from the harmful effects of traditional models of masculinity, which are socially constituted, and to develop more liberating models of manhood. For example, the NCFM claims that it wants to help men become more nurturing towards their children. While there is this kind of occasional shift from the traditional model of masculinity, overall the anti-feminist liberationist model of a re-constituted male identity, is not that different to traditional patriarchal models. The liberationists' idea of giving men more 'freedom' in their choice of lifestyle appears to be the reproduction of older ideas about a free-spirited male subject rejecting the demands of family and capitalist work patterns. Both Paul Hoch (1979) and Michael Kimmel (1996) expose the historical struggles between the 'playboy' or hedonistic model of male identity and the 'puritan' or 'corporate man' model of masculinity. Barbara Ehrenreich (1983) also noticed the increasing tendency of men in the 1970s and 1980s to reject the constraints of traditional family life.

The anti-feminist liberationists' cultivation of 'new' practices for men is limited because anti-feminist liberationist discourses are mainly concerned with campaigning for strengthening men's rights in a variety of arenas where men have traditionally had different rights to women. They campaign for an end to positive discrimination in the workplace in favour of women – men's right to a job over others. They demand that men be consulted on matters pertaining to their partner's use of contraception and abortion– men's control of women's bodies. Without concern for the development of responsible fatherhood or mothers' rights, they demand fathers' rights in terms of custody and access to children: in other words men's control and ownership of children. Without an analysis of power, the anti-feminist liberationist analysis of masculinity remains, for the most part, within existing discourses about men's rights; they just formulate these rights through attacks on feminism rather than with recourse to more traditional ideas about masculinities.

Profeminism with its analysis of the relationship between men's identities and men's power has a much broader conceptual field within which to interrogate men's identities. The anti-feminist liberationists only examine the constitution of men's traditional identities within culture; they fail to connect these identities to broader structures of power to examine the clear differentials between men and women's social positions. Profeminism similarly interrogates the constitution of masculinity and its effects on men but locates these effects within a much more critical gendered framework. However, the issues that emerge in anti-feminist liberationist discourses about the negative aspects of men's identities are also present in aspects of some profeminist discourses and, as later chapters will expose, these issues have been constituted in different ways by different profeminist writers.

Mythopoetic groups

Mythopoetic and spiritualist discourse on manhood draws heavily on the work of Carl Jung (see Hall and Norby 1993). Jungian psychology operates around the idea that psycho-spiritual health can be achieved through the analysis of certain cultural or spiritual archetypes. Archetypes are ideals and patterns of behaviour that exist in the collective consciousness. Mythopoetic and spiritualist writers use Jung's theory of archetypal forms to generate the notion of an authentic masculinity (for further analysis see Clatterbaugh 1990; Hagan 1992; Kimmel 1998). While several mythopoetic and spiritualist men would argue that they are primarily concerned with individual men's psychological health, their discourse operates around the same concerns as the other groups examined in this chapter.

Mythopoetic writers have developed different models of spiritualist practices for men (compare Rowan 1987 with Bly 1990). Forms of mythopoetic discourse and practice produce essentialist ideas about male identity. Like the groups discussed previously, some mythopoetic writers believe that modern manhood is in a state of crisis and they try to generate solutions to this crisis. While Clatterbaugh (1990: 87) characterises this approach as less political than that of the other men's groups, this discourse produces a variety of gendered and racial power-effects (Hagan 1992; Kimmel 1995 analyse these effects).

As noted, mythopoetic and spiritualist practitioners adopt different approaches to questions about masculinities. The following discussion is confined to examining the masculinist discourses of Robert Bly, an influential figure in developing mythopoetic approaches to masculinity.

Writers began to develop what has now become known as a mythopoetic and spiritualist discourse on masculinity in the 1970s. However, men's mythopoetic discourse did not really become popular until the 1990s. Spiritualism generally operates around a set of rituals that are designed to develop aspects of a person's subjectivity. Therefore spiritualism has an active, participatory element. Gender identity is not simply constituted through discourses but is worked on through physical practices that encourage the formation of a particular identity. Men perturbed by cultural changes in gender relationships have drawn on the spiritualist approach and have tailored this kind of discourse to their own concerns. Mythopoetic men do not tend to have formal group structures but meet and work on their identity through workshops, retreats and meetings.

Robert Bly (1990: x, 60–61), like Farrell, originally viewed feminism as a positive social movement. In the 1980s Bly became critical of the impact of feminism on modern men. He began to claim that feminism suppresses the masculine spirit, which Bly (1990) understands as the essence of manhood. Bly claims that a 'deep' masculine subjectivity exists inside every man. What exactly this 'deep masculinity' consists of is difficult to grasp in Bly's discourse. Bly appears to shift from conservative ideas about male identity in that he suggests that deep masculinity is not biologically based. In a statement that seems concerned with deconstructing biological theories of male identity Bly (1990: 234) states that 'geneticists have discovered recently that the genetic difference between men and women amounts to just over 3%. That isn't much'. At the same time Bly seems to believe that masculinity is biologically rooted. Bly (1990: 234) maintains that the difference between men and women 'exists in every cell of the body'. Bly therefore suggests that masculinity is not determined by biological forces such as hormones but is a product of a gendered spiritual essence rooted within men's bodies.

For Bly then men's subjectivity arises from a pre-discursive spiritual force that is somatically based. According to Bly, men's spirituality is therefore very different to women's. Bly claims that in order to understand 'deep masculinity' the differences between the 'male' and 'female spirit' must be examined. Masculinity or the 'male spirit', in Bly's (1990) best selling book *Iron John*, is equated with male values that are distinct from female values. Bly constructs these values as pre-discursive dimensions of the 'male' and 'female' self. These spiritual values, according to Bly, determine authentic masculinity and femininity.

The differences between men and women's subjectivity are finely spun in Bly's work. For example he claims that men and women have a different relationship to nature. 'Female spirituality' means that women seek to protect the earth. 'Male spirituality', in contrast, means that men are in tune with nature and the spiritual world. Bly's work associates masculinity with physical scars, manual work and with instrumental aggression. These are the physical representations of the 'male spirit'.

The connection of masculinity to these things by Bly is made automatically with no real discussion. What is clear is that Bly believes that there is some 'deep manhood' that is reflected at a material level in men's traditional practices. Apart from this Bly tells us very little about 'deep masculinity'. Bly claims that it is a positive force and that it is not inherently violent.

'Deep masculinity', according to Bly's theory, lies dormant within the 'male' subject until activated through experience. Masculinity, he claims, is something that has to be found and stimulated through particular practices and social arrangements; he (1990: 15) tells us that it 'does not just happen by itself; it does not happen just because we eat wheaties'. In order to develop an authentic manhood, the male subject must search for the 'deep masculinity' that is within him.

Bly believes that modern men are in crisis because they have become disconnected from their 'deep masculinity' and cannot find it in contemporary conditions. For Bly this has resulted in the feminisation of the modern man and he claims that this has had a negative impact on modern men. Bly (1990: 4) states that the young men who come to his meetings are often in tears within a few minutes of attending a mythopoetic seminar. For Bly this reflects the emotional problems that emerge if young men do not connect to their 'deep masculinity'.

One of the main problems for men in contemporary society, according to Bly, is that they are no longer initiated into masculinity and masculine values by other men. In modern society the bond and connection between younger and older men has been broken. Bly claims that the economic changes brought by the industrial revolution have almost dissolved older, more traditional relationships between boys and their fathers. This is because prior to the Industrial Revolution fathers and sons lived in close proximity to each other, with the father often teaching the son a trade. Bly claims that modern systems of production have destroyed the father's ability to pass on masculine values to the son. The modern father, Bly (1990: 19) writes, works away from home; this means that many fathers only see their sons for a few minutes each day. Bly's notion of a 'deep masculinity' is therefore very firmly connected to traditional forms of manhood and fatherhood.

Bly argues that the rise in single parenthood has meant that the post-60s generation of men are devoid of a 'male role' model. He (1990: 19) tells us that in days of old through 'hunting parties, in work that men did together in farms and cottages through local sports, older men spent much time with younger men and brought knowledge of male spirit and soul to them'.

With changes in production and the family these relationships between men, Bly tells us, no longer exist. Men, Bly claims, are therefore not being initiated into manhood by older men; instead women have taken over the role of bringing up boys and they cannot teach men manhood. Bly claims that the dominance of women in bringing up boys has not just created problems for men getting in touch with their deep masculine self. He (1990: 24) argues that overexposure to feminine values can leave boys with a wounded image of manhood. Bly (1990: 25) writes: 'If the son learns feeling primarily from the mother, then he will probably see his own masculinity from the feminine point of view as well. He may even pity it and want to reform it, or he may be suspicious of it and want to kill it'. Young men's wounded image of manhood, Bly claims, has manifested itself in both popular culture and politics which portray older men in negative ways. The father, he (1990: 92) claims, is rejected, imagined as a 'demonic figure' or 'the subject of ridicule'.

As a social force feminism has exacerbated these problems. For Bly feminists are correct to claim that men have had more power than women in society, but the creation of 'soft' men has been an unfortunate by-product of feminism's battle for equality. The problem is, as Bly constructs it, that young men have identified with these values and with women. Women, he (1990: 3) claims, reward 'receptive maleness,' while associating 'non-receptive maleness' with violence. Bly claims that now when he looks out over an audience:

> perhaps half the young males are what I would call soft. They're lovely, valuable people – I like them – they're not interested in harming the earth or starting wars. There's a gentle attitude toward life in their whole being and style of living . . . Here is a finely tuned man, ecologically superior to his father, sympathetic to the whole harmony of the universe, yet himself has little vitality to offer.
>
> (1990: 2–3)

The fading of the 'warrior', as Bly (1990: 156) puts it, contributes to the collapse of a civilised society and has left young men suffering tremendous emotional pain. Therefore Bly constructs a discourse of masculinity around the impact of feminism on men and frames two main aspects of modern manhood, fatherhood and men's emotional pain in post-feminist culture as problematic for men and for society.

Predictably, given his aim, as outlined above, Bly (1990: 18) argues that one of the main things that the modern man must do is to 'throw off all indoctrination and begin to discover for himself what the father is and what masculinity is'. First of all men must disassociate and separate from the feminine. Bly (1990: 89) tells us that 'fish and turtles are independent of the mother from the first day'. However, for the human male 'independence from the mother's womb world goes in agonisingly slow motion'.

Bly uses the technique of story telling to guide men through a process that will produce what he calls the positive traits and values of older forms of manhood. Bly uses the story of Iron John to produce an ideal of 'male' identity which is essentialist, constituted through a spiritualist discourse of sexual difference. In his book *Iron John* Bly (1990) outlines a set of practices that will return the 'male' subject to his true 'authentic manliness' represented by the figure Iron John. Separation from the mother, finding 'lost masculinity' and the concept of 'male wounding' are central themes. Men are wounded emotionally in different ways by their fathers and mothers. Mothers wound by rejecting masculinity, fathers through, for example, emotional distance and criticism. However despite wounding by the father, Bly suggests that men must identify with their fathers. This discourse of wounding has been integrated in to some forms of profeminism (Chapter 8).

Bly and other mythopoetics have also organised retreats to connect men to their masculinities. At these retreats men connect to certain symbols because these symbols stimulate masculine identity. This includes connecting to the 'ancient ancestors', drums and tribal songs. In order to connect to the 'ancient ancestors', which are, of course, in this context, 'male' ancient ancestors, men enter into practices such playing drums and chanting African songs learned from the movies. In meetings they tie red ribbons around their bodily scars, scars being another symbol of manhood (see Kimmel 1995).

Bly seeks to connect masculinity to existing models of manhood represented by older men. Although this model of masculinity is constituted through a mix of objects and ideas that have no intrinsic connection to masculinity, writers have noted how Bly appropriates symbols from traditional cultures (see Kimmel 1995). Clearly this strategy seeks to establish some image of authenticity around male identity, unsullied by the capitalist structures of late modernity.

The interrelationships between Bly's model of masculinity and traditional forms of masculinity are particularly evident in Bly's comments on men's violence towards women. While Bly claims that his vision of masculinity is not violent, he justifies domestic violence by a son against a mother in *Iron John* by claiming the son's violence was a natural response to this young boy's need for contact with a father figure. Also, when asked at one of his retreats what men should do when women challenge their ideas, Bly is reported to have responded that they should 'bust' these women 'in the mouth' (Chapple and Talbot 1990: 196).

Bly therefore seeks to fix masculine identity in the contemporary conditions which have reduced the ontological securities of men's identities and he does this through an anti-feminist and traditional framework. Bly is really suggesting to men that they have two alternatives: either they lose their traditional manhood and move in a profeminist direction to become 'soft' or they get over the harm that masculinity produces for men and re-iterate a traditional form of masculinity. The concept of wounding, therefore, has the potential effect of creating a stronger identification with normative models of manhood. Bly's discursive construction of a more involved fatherhood, if taken up by men, is also likely to have the effect of socialising boys more rigidly into this model of manhood (Kimmel 1995).

Bly's discourse also appears to have the potential effect of producing a modern man more capable of defending his traditional manhood. Bly's discourse provides men with discursive legitimisation to resist the demands of feminism and of individual women for change in gender relationships and men's behaviour. What Bly is saying to men is, identify with the Iron John, the wild man, your masculinity, and you will be able to stand up to women and preserve your traditional male identity. This is clear when we read the following statement by Bly:

> The man experiences an angry woman; but something in the angry woman's malice introduces him perhaps for the first time to the Rageful One, the Dark Side of the Moon, the ogre who lives on the back side of the moon with bat wings and ripped-apart birds ... The only solution to the power of the witch is for the young man to develop energy as great as hers, as harsh, as wild, as shrewd, as clear in its desire.
>
> (1990: 77–78)

Bly's discourse also seems to generate an identity for men amid the loss of the traditional symbols of manhood. As traditional male identity is a fiction produced through particular discourses its symbols must be discursively produced and re-invented in the new conditions of late capitalism. Traditionally masculinity has been associated with manual work, sports such as hunting and the rugged outdoors. Many of the men interested in Bly's work cannot associate themselves with such activities as many are middle class men living in suburbia. Bly's mythopoetic myths and practices produce representations of masculinity by appropriating symbols and practices of older cultures. Michael Schwalbe (1995: 45) reports one man at a retreat telling him that only men can connect to the drum: women cannot. The tragedy is, of course, that the men Schwalbe interviewed cannot play drums; even more tragic is that the significance of this does not seem to register with them.

The potential effect of connecting to the drums and the 'ancient ancestors' is to produce the idea that there is a 'true' masculine self that must be found which potentially directs men away from reflecting on the concerns of feminism. While Bly does not treat gay men's identity as pathological, he does not see this identity as representing difference and seeks to tie it to the archetype of the wild man. By doing so Bly tries to sideline the pluralism of masculinities; the effect of this is the production of a sharper constitution of sexual difference.

The mythopoetic movement's essentialist discourse on gender identity combined with its tendency to homogenise men into a unitary category constituted through the theory of a common spiritual masculine essence within all men means that many of the possibilities for critically examining men's identities and re-inventing them are closed off. Profeminism with its theory of men's identities as plural, shifting and socially constituted explores the aspects of masculinity that essentialist standpoints about masculinity prevent.

In contrast mythopoetic discourse and practices provides a mythology of masculinity that leads to men avoiding a critical engagement with their identity and its connection to gender inequalities. If men like Bly and Farrell really want to understand men's identity they need to examine relations of power between men and women. However, as it is unlikely that either of these men will brush the dust off their old feminist texts and rethink their approach to masculinity, profeminism remains the only form of men's gendered politics that seeks to engage with the networks of power that produce gendered identities. Despite the clear differences between profeminism and the regressive discourses about masculinity discussed above, some feminists have been suspicious of the new profeminist politics of masculinity.

6 The Problematic of Men and Feminism

Men's identity and feminist politics

Clowns to the left of me,
Jokers to the right,
Here I am stuck in the middle with you.

(Stealers Wheel)

While profeminism seems markedly more politically progressive compared with the men's groups examined in the last chapter, a number of feminists have viewed profeminist subject positions as problematic. This chapter outlines critical feminist engagements with profeminism and develops a framework for analysing the particular concerns raised by profeminism's style of politics as practiced by a dominant identity. The chapter concentrates on the problems that have emerged in profeminist models of personal and public politics. It also examines the contentious issues of linking men's subjectivity and experience to oppositional gender politics, and charts the relationship of these categories to gendered power and feminist theory and practice.

'Forced entry' and 'gender tourism'

One of the first academic discussions of profeminism was organised by the Modern Language Association and was held in Washington in 1984. The MLA brought feminist women and self-defined profeminists together to discuss the possibility of 'men doing feminism'. These discussions were later published in a collection of essays entitled *Men in Feminism* (Jardine and Heath 1987). The loaded title of the collection reflected the general thrust of the feminist contributors' analysis of what was defined as profeminism. Their response was generally hostile. The consistent theme that emerged in the feminist discussions of men in feminism was that it represented a form of 'forced entry' and 'defilement' (Morris 1987: 173–81). The feminist contributors also queried the reasons for men's sudden turn to feminist theory. Some feminists suggested that the declining legitimacy of traditional critical frameworks has meant that feminism has come to represent a new and productive body of theory that 'male' theorists can utilise for their own analytical purposes.

For example, Rosi Braidotti (1987: 234–35) argued forcefully that academic men have appropriated feminist thought in ways that are largely instrumental. Braidotti argued that academic profeminists appropriate feminism, its concepts and ideas, but lack commitment to the ideals of feminist politics. She writes:

> It must be very uncomfortable to be a male, white, middle class intellectual at a time in history when so many minorities and oppressed groups are speaking up for themselves; at a time when the hegemony of the white knowing subject is crumbling. Lacking the historical experience of oppression on the basis of sex, they paradoxically lack a minus . . . it must be very painful indeed to have no option other than being the empirical referent of the historical oppressor of women.
>
> (1987: 234)

A theme that developed in the *Men in Feminism* collection operated around the idea that profeminism is a form of fetishism (see Braidotti 1987: 116–32). Braidotti claimed that profeminist fetishism abstracts feminist theory from the political context of gender relationships to become merely an object that has theoretical utility for those men employing it. Hence Stephen Heath (1987: 4) asked, 'Is it possible to wonder whether there is not in male feminism . . . always potentially a pornographic effect?' (for alternative perspectives see Digby 1998).

Therefore, for these feminist critics of profeminism, having a relationship with feminism does not necessarily move men beyond exploitative relationships with women; rather it can reproduce forms of gender power through the medium of men's appropriation of feminism. Such claims about the nature of profeminism resonate with the concerns of other feminists and profeminists who have also examined the effects of men's turn to feminist frameworks within the institutional arena of the university.

For Victoria Robinson and Diane Richardson (1996: 186), the rise of profeminist men within academia has the potential to de-radicalise and dilute feminist teaching and research. Profeminism, they claim, has led to the emergence of new academic areas, namely men's studies and gender studies. This change of name opens the way for men to move in on feminist teaching. They argue that profeminism constitutes a threat in the form of a 'take-over' of women's studies courses by men. This echoes Braidotti's claim that men:

> circle around women's studies departments in crisis-stricken Arts Faculties, knowing that here's one of the few areas of the Academy which is still expanding financially and in terms of students . . . They play the academic career game with great finesse, knowing the rule about feminist separatism yet ignoring it.
>
> (1987: 235–36)

In view of these kinds of concerns about men's movement onto feminist territory, Moore (1988) has argued that men may be acting as gendered tourists through feminism. She suggests that men may be finding feminist ideas attractive to 'play' with but continue to distance themselves from the more politically orientated feminist goal of gender equality. Modleski (1991) raises another issue in relation to men's turn towards an awareness of gender issues. She claims that men's turn to feminism as a medium to examine masculinities may have the effect of returning men to the centre stage of politics and theory. Furthermore she maintains that men's appropriation of feminism may allow men to defuse the 'power' of feminism by integrating it within their conceptual fields, thereby reducing feminism's critical potential in relation to men's power.

Machiavellian deployments of profeminist identities have also occurred outside of the academic environments. The Jungian profeminist writer John Rowan (1987) relays the story of one man who became involved in spiritualism and joined a feminist spiritualist group. The man in question told Rowan that spiritualism was helping him combat sexism. When Rowan talked to the women in the coven to which the man belonged, he found that the man had had sex with every woman in the group including two women who identified as lesbians. Two of the women had become pregnant including one of the gay women.

Feminists have also been concerned about the activities of men during the White Ribbon Campaign. Spark (1994) claims that some of the men involved in wearing the white ribbon, which symbolised men's opposition to violence against women, had been previously involved in violence against women. Other critics also suggested that some men were wearing white ribbons because it increased their chances of getting dates with women (Goldrick-Jones 2002). The issues that feminists raise in relation to the commitment of profeminists, and the more general manipulation of feminism by men are serious issues that analysts of profeminism should be concerned about.

However as the next chapters will show, many profeminists have given their energies and commitment to feminism and have attempted to think through and actively pursue non-exploitative relationships with feminism and other gendered groups. Profeminists have implemented NSM strategies across the public and private arenas of gender relationships in attempts to contribute to the attainment of feminist goals and to reformulate men's identities in feminist directions. These strategies, however, have raised their own set of problems. Formulating profeminist politics through NSM strategies raises issues about the effectiveness of NSM models of political engagement across the terrain of identity as discussed in Chapter 3. Some profeminist deployments of strategies associated with NSMs that orientate around the level of personal explorations of identity raise other concerns about the effects of certain forms of profeminism (see Chapter 8).

The rest of this chapter assesses the kind of problems that emerge in profeminist political strategies and applies some of the insights of the post-structuralist analysis of subjectivity to frame these problems conceptually. The remaining chapters of the book examine how key profeminist writers and activists have formulated and responded to the issues raised by profeminist practice and theory.

Personal politics

As already detailed profeminism, like other contemporary social movements, theorises power as operating at macro-levels and also at the very personal level of identity, lifestyle and personal ethics. However, unlike other contemporary radical movements that expose how power operates to subjugate identity categories such as women and/or alternative sexualities, profeminism seeks to expose how men's identities are involved in producing gendered power effects. Profeminism's concern with changing men's identities at the level of everyday life has led to political practices that are designed to expose how men are constituted as subjects that engage in oppressive gender behaviour towards others and also how masculinity constitutes men in ways that are detrimental to men.

Self-analysis of men's identity within a feminist framework has been one of the main strategies that profeminists have employed to engage with the social constitution of men's identities and the possibilities of changing those identities in ways that support the feminist ideal of gender equality. Different models of personal change have developed within profeminism (e.g. Rowan 1987; Seidler 1997; Pease 2000). Specific models of profeminist explorations of men's personal involvement in the reproduction of gender power have different degrees of connection to political action outside of the boundaries of personal exploration and change (compare Stoltenberg 1993; Seidler 1997). However in general these strategies involve men articulating their oppressive practices and their experiences of oppressing others. Strands of profeminism have also developed that explore men's negative experiences of masculinities in their everyday lives and in their relationships with others. This kind of exploration of men's identities and experiences has been used to generate forms of profeminist knowledge about men's identities that inform strategies for changing those identities.

This kind of self-analysis, as Chapter 4 illustrated, is a common practice in NSMs. As already discussed in Chapter 4, the deployment of therapeutic and consciousness-raising practices by other movements such as the women's movement have raised issues about the relationship between personal explorations of identity and NSM agendas for wider structural and macro-level change. Some feminists have argued that practices of consciousness-raising within the women's movement have distracted feminists from struggles for structural changes across the terrain of gender inequality and have reduced gender inequalities to personal problems. Segal (Segal 1999: 227) has argued, for example, that some feminists have replaced 'what they describe as their former "hardened" language of politics, with a "cosier" language of feelings'.

The issues that have arisen in relation to the political effects of group based personal explorations of identity within NSMs, and the concerns that surround the practices of consciousness-raising are amplified in profeminist politics because of men's dominant gender positioning. Some feminists have suggested that men's explorations of their identity through therapy or consciousness-raising are not only apolitical but actually lead to the reproduction of patriarchal standpoints. Hester (1984: 34) claims that the group of profeminist men she studied used group analysis of men's identities to 'put women down,' reproduce men's self-interests and to advance men's power in the arena of heterosexuality. Therapeutic strategies in profeminist men's groups may then, create new forms of gendered power dynamics.

The development of co-dependency groups have also been singled out for criticism by feminists. Co-dependency groups employ the principles of support groups, such as Alcoholics Anonymous, and are based around a 12-step programme very similar to those used in groups designed to support people with addictions. However, unlike addiction groups, co-dependency participants work on 'dysfunctional' relations with others, especially romantic partners. These groups are usually open to both men and women. Feminists have argued that these groups frame traits associated with women, such as the desire to please others and low self-esteem, as pathological (Walters 1995: 184). This type of group practice has also been criticised for encouraging men and women to seek personal solutions to structural problems through self-analysis and individual change (184–85).

Critiques of therapy and consciousness-raising expose the concerns that surround certain forms of 'work' on identity and subjectivity within NSMs and profeminism in particular. However the work of other analysts of NSMs caution against reducing these kinds of strategies to distractions from political action. Melucci (1989:60) has suggested that in times of movement latency, when opportunities do not exist for NSMs to effect broader political structures though, for example, public campaigns, group and individual interrogations of identities may mean that NSMs act as 'cultural laboratories' that generate oppositional discourses and models of identities. When movements are less active in public campaigns more introspective forms of political activity help maintain a constituency of support for the movement. Furthermore, oppositional ideas developed during periods of political inaction can inform the movements' agenda when it again becomes more publicly active. Taylor's (1996) study of a women's post-partum support group illustrates these processes in action. Practices of emotional self-disclosure by the women involved in this group became the discursive material that later provided a foundation for public activism around the issues that the support group gave rise to in relation to women's post-partum experiences.

Those who have employed strategies of consciousness-raising dispute the claim that these practices are intrinsically apolitical. They suggest that political consciousness-raising within Second Wave feminism was not about adapting personal behaviour or primarily about personal goals or development. Instead, as Perl and Abardanell (1979: 24) put it 'political awareness is the purpose of consciousness-raising, personal growth the gravy'. Furthermore these feminists suggest that there are variations in consciousness-raising practices. They argue (1979: 24) if the focus shifts from political awareness to personal growth then 'the group is not doing feminist political consciousness-raising'. As Part II will illustrate, strands within profeminism have also adopted this position on the formulation of consciousness-raising strategies.

Certainly studies such as Taylor's suggest that therapeutic groups, consciousness-raising and discussion groups that engage with identities may be important aspects in NSM politics. Therefore it is important not to dismiss these practices as simply apolitical discussions of 'silly stuff'. Instead it seems important to analyse, as Taylor does, how these practices are formulated within certain movement contexts and their effects within movements. However when these practices are analysed within profeminism, given feminist concerns about the potential benefits such practices may generate for men, it is important to focus on how these practices may operate to support men's dominant social positions.

The next two chapters in particular examine profeminist strategies across the arena of group-based analysis of men's identities. These chapters expose the different models of personal change that have been developed for men by prominent profeminist writers and activists. This exploration of these models of personal change, as subsequent chapters expose, vary within profeminism and raise a diverse range of issues about the micro and personal level of politics within the movement.

However such an analysis is not possible without attention to the category of experience within profeminism. Much self and group analysis of men's identities within profeminism operates around men's disclosure of their experiences as socially constituted subjects within broader networks of power. The examination and disclosure of men's experiences have been deployed by profeminists to develop forms of oppositional knowledges around men's identities which then become the basis for profeminist models for changing men's identities in non-patriarchal ways. Some feminists have contended that men lack the experiences that generate feminist knowledge. The next section considers this claim. It examines some of the ideas that emerged about experience, gender and resistance in some forms of radical feminism. Radical feminism is a diverse strand of feminism supporting a range of perspectives. However the work of some radical feminists discussed below formulated influential theories about the relationships between women's experience and feminist knowledge.[1]

Profeminism, experience and gender politics

The relationship between men's experiences and profeminist knowledge is contentious because some feminist writers have suggested that feminist knowledge is grounded in women's experiences of oppression. This constitution of women's experience as the ground of feminist knowledge and politics suggested that as men do not share women's gendered experiences of oppression, men lack the epistemological foundations of feminist resistance. Aware that men's and women's gendered experiences are different, profeminists, as the preceding section indicated, have nevertheless employed the concept of men's experiences to develop strategies of gendered resistance to normative gender identities and normative gendered relationships. To consider the issue of men's experiences in profeminism, traditional feminist accounts of the category of gendered experience need to be examined and considered.

Modern feminism was built around the idea that women, regardless of their many differences, suffer a common experience of oppression and therefore constitute a collectively subjugated group. Emerging out of that recognition, contemporary feminism has explored the possibility of articulating a politics of resistance through the category of women's experience. A number of influential feminists have identified women's experiences as the epistemological basis of feminist politics (Alpert 1973; Daly 1973, 1979, 1984; Rich 1976; MacKinnon 1987). These writers suggest that women's experience under patriarchal social conditions gives them access to a particular standpoint on the world that challenges the corrupt and oppressive values and practices of current social systems. The work of Rich (1976) reflects the assumptions of these traditional standpoint theories. She argues that women's painful experiences of gender subjugation provide them with a counter-epistemology that challenges the logic of patriarchal systems.

While some standpoint theorists view women's experience as potentially subversive, they correspondingly encourage the idea that men's experience is fundamentally patriarchal. Basing feminist resistance in a unique female experience suggests, by implication, that men, because they have no personal experience of gender oppression, lack the experiential basis to develop an oppositional feminist consciousness. Hence, some standpoint theories tend to erect a bar to men engaging in feminist politics.

This barrier appears all the more unsurpassable when suggestions are made that men's experience may be biologically based. For example, as critics (Echols 1989) have noted, MacKinnon's work suggests that men's oppressive sexual practices may be an outcome of their biological make-up. Similarly, Daly (1979: 59) argues that men's biological inability to give birth lies at the root of their oppression of women as they envy and seek to control women's unique life-giving capacity. Men, then, according to these accounts are doomed to replicate the mechanisms of gender oppression and domination. Men and women are viewed as representing two separate epistemic or experiential communities.

The foundational use of the category of experience as a ground for feminist politics and knowledge has been subjected to sustained criticism. Black feminists and working class women have exposed how appeals to a common female experience involved constituting women's experience from a white, middle class perspective that excluded the experiences of other women. As the notion of a unitary female experience has increasingly broken apart, feminists influenced by post-structuralism have argued that feminism must understand gendered experience as a multiple product of intersecting modalities of power (Haraway 1991; Butler 1990).

The post-structuralist deconstruction of humanist and biological conceptions of the subject has also resulted in a general shift by feminists towards theorisations of gender and sex as cultural rather than biological creations. Many women from different schools of feminist thought have rejected the idea that their experience or standpoint is defined by female biology. The post-structuralist theorisation of subjectivity as culturally constituted has also deconstructed the idea that there is a foundational epistemology from which feminism can gain a complete understanding of the world (Haraway 1991). Feminism has increasingly understood knowledge as partial, contextual and situated.

Despite these advances in theory and feminism's recognition of the complexity of the category of experience, critics of profeminism have continued to argue that male experience bars men from developing a feminist consciousness and feminist knowledge. So while women's experience has been refigured, reworked and questioned, some feminists have insulated men's experiences from this general rethinking of the category of gendered experience. This is evident if the theorisation of men's experience in certain forms of feminist theory is examined.

For example Bart et al. (1991), quoted in Ewing and Schacht (1998), assert that 'one must inhabit a female body to have the experiences that make one a feminist' (p. 131). The experiential bar to contemporary profeminism therefore revolves around the claim that men's social position isolates them from gender oppression. The idea of a singular organic female standpoint emerging from experience has been rethought, and it is also important to rethink the idea of a singular organic experiential 'male' standpoint.

Other feminists, and several of the profeminist perspectives examined in Part II, have reconsidered the issue of men's experiences and feminist politics. Bell hooks, an important figure in the exposure by black feminists of the exclusions that arise from the universalising of some women's experiences, has also attacked feminist refusals of profeminism (hooks 1998). Hooks argues that feminism should not set up any barrier to profeminism but should welcome profeminist men as allies in the struggle for gender equality.

Hooks explains that women who have suffered class or racial oppression have generally been more open to the idea of profeminism and traditionally have been keener to form political alliances with men. These feminists have been more open to claims that men are also oppressed because of their class or racial identity. Hooks points out that black feminists and feminists involved in socialist politics have therefore rarely supported feminist separateness. For hooks, the rejection of men's participation in feminist goals is a white 'bourgeoisie' feminist response. White middle class women, hooks claims, have not been prepared to examine the way that men can also suffer oppression. According to hooks, this is because these women do not suffer this kind of oppression.

Hooks highlighted the tendency of white, middle class feminists to prioritise their gender oppression and to ignore other forms of oppression. She points out that while working class and black women share experiences of oppression with men, white feminists lack this connection. This, hooks explains, is why black women and socialist women have bonded politically with men; they share similar experiences and similar political views (266). These women, hooks tells us, are much more orientated towards alliances with men. Middle class white women however, in contrast, have been uninterested in men's experiences of oppression because it has no relationship to their understanding of oppression as gendered (274).

Hooks attacks feminist separatism on two counts. She contends that it is another form of feminist exclusion that has operated against black women in the past and now operates against men. She argues that feminism should recognise that men suffer under patriarchy but not in a way that justifies sexism or fails to place responsibility on men for changing it (270). She also views separatism as negative for feminism in practical terms (278). Hooks argues that because men are the 'primary agents' in the perpetuation of sexism they must be active in its eradication and must assume responsibility for it (278). In other words, she claims that if the oppression of women is to end, then men need to reform themselves. She contends that when men have taken on their share of the struggle for gender equality they should be viewed as 'comrades in struggle' (270).

Doris Ewing and Steven Schacht (1998: 1) agree with hooks that there is no intrinsic barrier to 'men doing feminism'. These writers believe that the definition of feminism can be expanded 'to include co-operative ventures between men and women working together to bring about positive social change'. Their claim is that feminism must be based on 'respect for all people' (9). They call for a feminism that is inclusive and supports the interests of people coming from different social locations, including men (9; 10). Feminism, they claim, by demonising men, assumes an unhelpful and alienating ideology. Echoing hooks, they argue that this makes 'co-operative ventures nearly impossible' (9).

Recent studies of masculinity suggest that men's subjectivity is affected by a number of variables and cross-cutting identities and is therefore diverse (see e.g. Connell 1995). This insight is reflected in the attempts of feminists from minority groups, such as hooks, to connect the experiences of oppression suffered by men within their social group to feminist politics. This work exposes men's experiences as diverse rather than unitary. Furthermore, as hooks (1998) argues, men's experience of racial discrimination may act as a bridge to connect them to the feminist cause.

This intervention by hooks still, however, does not deal fully with the issue of men's development of feminist knowledge through white, middle class men's experiences. However, post-structuralism may offer a way of reformulating the relationship between men's identities, men's experiences and feminist knowledge and practice. The central assumption that informs post-structuralist theories of gender is that gendered identities are not intrinsic to the subject (Butler 1990). Rather they are effects of the cultural matrix within which the subject is located. This theorisation of gender subjectivity is supported by a broader epistemological framework that operates around the claim that the world has no intrinsic meaning (Foucault 1970: 1972). Rather, the meaning, significance and value that come to be ascribed to aspects of the world are ascribed culturally. The claim is that symbolic and discursive systems do not reflect the intrinsic or natural qualities of things themselves.

For post-structuralists, the human subject is also devoid of any pre-discursive meaning. Subjectivity, according to this account, has no intrinsic form that is naturally expressed nor does the subject have recourse to any pre-discursive understanding of itself that naturally unfolds through its maturation in the world. This makes its identity and knowledge of itself and its world dependent on the field of cultural intelligibility within which it is located. Without this field of meaning, the subject would be unable to delineate itself as a separate subject or engage in the world in any meaningful way (Butler 1990, p.143).

This theory suggests that gender identity, like other forms of identity, is an effect of a particular cultural field of intelligibility that creates the category of gender. The power-effects of this field are therefore the production of normative, rigid and dichotomous gender identities. If gender identity is a culturally constituted category then men's experiences and consciousness cannot be understood as biologically based or organic.

According to post-structuralist accounts of gender identity, gendered experiences are the effects of discourses that produce gendered subjects at the material level. For example, gendered practices in the workplace, in the family and in sport constitute particular masculinities subjectively and somatically. As Joan Scott (1992: 26) states, 'it is not individuals who have experience, but subjects who are constituted through discourse'. We never own our identity and we never own our experience because there is no point from within the self from which these categories 'naturally' emerge. Rather subjectivity and experience are practices that we reiterate that do not inherently belong to us. Normative gender experiences are culturally constituted practices that generate subjectivity. Men's gender consciousness, their ethical relationship to their gender identity, is also culturally constituted within particular discursive formations that produce normative ideals about normal or legitimate gender behaviour. Consciousness is an effect of the social but also generative of subjectivity. According to this theory of subjectivity consciousness is a category in process within changing and conflictual fields of power that support different interpretative frameworks.

To explain further, for radical constructionists like Butler, the reiteration of gendered practices and standpoints is never a secure process but is always open to contestation and re-figuration. It is through this theory of subjectivity as a process open to contestation that post-structuralism advances our understanding of the relationship between men's experiences and gendered consciousness. This theoretical framework replaces an over-determined theory of men's experience and consciousness which posits both as fixed and inherently patriarchal with a dynamic reading of both categories as contingent, unstable and shifting.

For post-structuralists the formation of gender identity does not occur within a fixed field of static ideological and structural power relationships as traditional feminist theories of power suggest. For example, Rich (1976) tends to see gender power as monolithic and all encompassing. In contrast, these theorists re-read gender power as dynamic, always shifting and reconfiguring as contestations emerge around identity at different times. Within this field traditional discourses may be maintained or become redundant and new knowledges and discourses about identity emerge (Foucault 1970; 1972; 1980). This fluidity within the field of power relationships means that identity is often a site of discursive struggle. This struggle can have many effects, however; as Foucault (1986) has shown in his study of Greek ethics, one effect is the emergence of different ethical relationships to the self that produce different types of subjectivity.

Therefore, it seems clear that any analysis of men's experiences and consciousness needs to examine these categories within their political and historical contexts and explore the struggles that often emerge around identities. The traditional claim that experience determines consciousness precludes such an analysis and this is why it can tell us very little about the relationship between men's experiences, men's consciousness and feminist knowledge. It ignores the mechanisms, through which experience and consciousness are produced and reproduced, largely because it perceives it as fixed, unitary and stable.

The last chapter illustrated how men's interpretation of their experience differed in relation to different types of men's groups. For example, the mythopoetic discourses of men's experiences as pre-determined subjects differed from the liberationists' theory of men's experiences as social subjects. Therefore in the current context of gender relationships wherein traditional and post-traditional discourses and practices intersect there has been a discursive struggle around men's experience that has engendered multiple interpretations of men's experience. Some interpretations of men's experiences, as Chapter 5 exposed, act in anti-feminist ways.

Profeminism deploys men's experiences in a different fashion. In profeminism men's experience is deployed through the practices of articulating and critically reflecting on men's experiences of the world. Men's experience therefore becomes part of the material for profeminist knowledge and critical gendered frameworks (see Ashe 2004). However readings of those experiences are not predetermined by men's identities. Instead those experiences are interpreted through feminist frameworks. However, shifting analytically to such an interpretation of profeminism's approach to men's experiences does not mean that men's experience is only deployed in a fashion that effectively challenges gender power across the arena of men's identities in profeminist politics. Experiential exclusivity, as Chapter 8 illustrates, can emerge in forms of profeminism that distance interrogations of men's experience from critical modes of feminist analysis. Furthermore, as Butler (1990) reminds us, foundational deployments of identity to construct political knowledges may reproduce the very categories of identity that support the power relationships that movements seek to undermine. As subsequent chapters expose, different deployments of men's experience in profeminism have led to different power-effects.

However, again, it is important to note that these outcomes are not pre-determined by men's consciousness but are created through discursive frameworks that can be interrogated and questioned. When discourses about men's experiences and identities are examined in subsequent chapters it will become evident that men's experience is a highly contested and highly political category within profeminism; it is not a category that can be understood with reference to the epistemological bar. Rather it becomes the malleable material of politics within this movement. Instead of constituting barriers to the generation of feminist knowledge through the category of experience, the next chapters illustrate the need to focus on the political articulation of profeminist politics and practice in relation to the category of experience.

The deployment of the category of men's experience generates complex forms of political practice. Furthermore, given the criticisms that have been constructed in relation to personal forms of politics by NSMs and the concerns that surround men's deployment of their gendered experience as a basis for oppositional gender politics, it seems important to examine public action campaigns by profeminists. As these kinds of campaigns rest much more on the experiences and knowledges of women and feminism, public campaigns offer another form of oppositional gendered practice for men.

Profeminism and public campaigns

Profeminist public campaigns seem to avoid the issues raised by more reflective, micro-level forms of personal politics. These campaigns also often reflect issues of power raised by the women's movement such as men's violence towards women and the sexual assault of women. Therefore much of the foundational knowledge for these campaigns emerged from women's critical interpretation and articulation of their experiences of men's violence. Furthermore men's involvement with such issues seems to deconstruct the notion that gender violence is a 'woman's issue' and makes it the concern of the broader community.

However some feminists have been critical of men's engagement in public expressions of politics around issues of domestic and sexual violence. It has been suggested that the men involved in these campaign 'take over'. As Kimmel (1998: 62) frames it 'profeminist men, like the cavalry come to the rescue of the damsel in distress'. They say: 'Thanks for bringing all this patriarchy stuff to our attention . . . We'll take it from here'. There have also been accusations that men pursue 'glory' through public profeminist campaigns and subsequently the welfare of women takes second place (Goldrick-Jones 2002) in these articulations of gender politics.

For example, Spark (1994) argues that during the White Ribbon Campaign the organisers were more concerned with extending office space and increasing campaign funds than with supporting existing women's centres that had been providing support for women long before the Montreal murders. The next chapters will show how profeminists have responded to the concerns surrounding issues of funding and accountability to feminism in profeminist politics by developing particular models of profeminist practice.

However other concerns surround profeminist public campaigns. Chapter 4 illustrated the problems surrounding micro-level politics and this chapter has shown how these problems emerge in profeminist practice. However some theorists have argued that micro-level and marginal deployments of identity politics may be more radical than public campaigning and lobbying because micro-level forms of politics are often more difficult to assimilate (see Buechler 2000 for discussion).

Feminist explorations of the WRC suggest that the campaign became diluted, non-threatening and apolitical. Spark (1994) writes that: 'perhaps this explains why the WRC, unlike feminist organizations, can get corporate donations of office space in the prestigious Toronto Eaton's Centre, as well as why they were given cash, furniture, office equipment, and computers'. Overall she notes how easily the White Ribbon Foundation 'blended into the politics and landscape of corporate Canada'.

Furthermore Spark claims that the campaign gradually became limited to a single issue rather than a broader critique of patriarchy and targeted capitalist corporations for funding. Spark's critique of the WRC again raises concerns about the personal/public divide in terms of political activism which is explored further in the next chapters. What seems to be clear at this point is that neither public nor private politics can be assessed without an examination of their actual articulation or effects within specific movements (see Profeministimiehet as an alternative profeminist approach to campaigns around domestic violence).

More specifically profeminism has also raised the issue of how campaigns deploy and are received through existing gender frames. Chapters 3 and 4 suggested that progressive and traditional forms of gender power dynamically intersect in contemporary cultures. Furthermore Chapter 4 highlighted Butler's claim that using identity as a foundation for politics often involves some kind of re-iteration of that identity and its power-effects. Therefore profeminist movement participants are located within institutional and discursive contexts that mediate how their political activities are framed. This creates issues for profeminist activism because the media can be more responsive, for example to the 'new male experts' on domestic violence which pushes women, their campaigning and their standpoints onto the sidelines (see Spark 1994). The deployment of profeminism within contexts of gendered power relationships means that the signification of profeminist politics is not entirely under the control of those engaged in this form of political activism but activists can certainly try to respond to issues concerning how their campaigns are publicly framed. Again, as the next chapters expose, profeminists have had to consider these issues.

This chapter has detailed and evaluated some of the concerns that specific feminist writers have formulated in response to the development of profeminist politics. Profeminism's reaction and response to these issues means that the field of profeminist politics has become one of discussion and contention about the possible effects of NSM styles of politics and about men's ability to support or participate in the feminist movement. Part II of this book examines these debates and exposes the different conceptions of subjectivity, agency and NSM politics that have emerged within profeminist scholarship and activism.

Part 2

Power and Resistance

7 John Stoltenberg

The politics of refusal

> Only in acts with consequences to others is manhood made flesh, and so long as manhood is believed to be worth proving, and the game worth playing, the code of the pack will determine who wins and who loses.
>
> Stoltenberg (2000: xxiv)

Stoltenberg has been a significant figure in profeminist politics. He was a high profile member of NOMAS until he left the organisation in 1991. The reasons for Stoltenberg's exit from NOMAS are discussed below. While a member of NOMAS, Stoltenberg founded the organisation Men Against Pornography in New York and was chair of the NOMAS Task Group on Pornography. One initiative that emerged from this task force was the Brother-Storm movement which brought men together across North America to campaign against rape and men's violence towards women (Goldrick-Jones 2002: 138).

Stoltenberg's academic background includes philosophy, English and theology. He was a managing editor from 1981 to 1991 of three US women's magazines: *Essence*, *Working Women* and *Lear's*. Stoltenberg has written two books on masculinity. The first, *Refusing to be a Man* (1990) analyses men's identities, gender power and inequality, and puts forward a cogent case for the appropriation of an anti-pornography agenda by profeminist men. *The End of Manhood* (2000) continued to consider similar issues to *Refusing to be a Man* but shifted the analysis of men's identities and power more firmly on to the arena of men's interpersonal relationships and the power effects of those relationships. *Refusing to be a Man* outlines Stoltenberg's philosophical standpoint on men's identity, gender power and sexuality. The structure and style of *The End of Manhood* is different in that this book parodies the self-help genre in masculinities literature. In this respect the book includes a satire of Bly's masculine archetype Iron John.

Pornography and violence against women have been the central targets of Stoltenberg's profeminist politics. He has been a highly vocal, visible and public campaigner against both aspects of gender power. Regardless of the different standpoints on pornography within the feminist community, it is difficult to doubt Stoltenberg's commitment to feminist politics. Indeed, as discussed below, some of his profeminist critics claim that Stoltenberg is too welded to feminist perspectives, especially the standpoint of radical feminist writers such as Dworkin (e.g. 1974; 1981; 1982; 1987) and MacKinnon (e.g. 1987; 1989). Heavily influenced by radical feminists, especially Dworkin, Stoltenberg's analysis of masculinity and his formulation of strategies of profeminism is viewed, by some writers, as representing the radical feminist strand of profeminist politics (Clatterbaugh 1990; Messner 1997).

This chapter explores Stoltenberg's model of profeminist politics and examines his analysis of men's identity, his constitution of profeminist knowledge and his formulation of activism. By analysing Stoltenberg's model of profeminist politics across these categories, the chapter assesses Stoltenberg's fusion of NSM strategy and men's feminist engagements.

Masculinity does not exist

For Stoltenberg (2000: xiv) gender is: 'a social construction. It gets made up. It is collective make believe'. This theory of gender identity means that Stoltenberg 'empties' men's identities of any intrinsic subjectivity and theorises masculinities as cultural products. For Stoltenberg masculinity is the term that describes men's socially constituted subjectivities and practices. There is, he claims, no prediscursive gender identity. Stoltenberg argues that men's identities have been constituted and are reproduced in ways that oppress, injure and limit the rights of women. Believing that masculinity is a 'mask', Stoltenberg (1990; 2000) documents the effects of men's traditional identities on women and men themselves. He engages in a discourse that attempts to exploit the indeterminacy of men's identities to change those identities beyond 'patriarchal' constitutions of gender. Stoltenberg (1990) calls on men to 'refuse' manhood and he looks forward to the deconstruction of the concept of men's identity and the discourses and practices of sexual difference that constitute it.

Stoltenberg theorises men's identities through a radical constructionist framework. However he does not adopt the non-normative stance associated with some forms of radical constructionist analysis (see Foucault 1980a; 1985; 1986 as an alternative). Stoltenberg instantiates a moral framework to guide the reconstitution of subjects defined as men. For Stoltenberg post-structuralism leads to a theory of gender as:

> putting in an appearance. It is signs and signifiers with no intrinsic substance. It is drag, dress-up or other camouflage ... It is an art form ... the public and private face of gender is ... an aesthetic ... so many academics are pursuing the study of gender as an aesthetic ...
>
> (2000 xiv-xv)

He argues that inquiry into the ethics of gender has been discouraged by the post-structuralist engagements with identity as an effect of signification. Stoltenberg contends that politics must be involved in interrogating morality. He (2000: xvi) maintains that this kind of interrogation requires an analysis of acts and consequences. It is debatable whether studies of gender as a process of signification through post-structuralist frameworks fully reflects the effects of post-structuralist methodologies on feminist interrogations of gender (see Ashe 1999, Ashe 2006a; 2006b; 2000c). Foucault in particular prioritises a critical engagement with the morality and norms of identity constitution; albeit in a different fashion to Stoltenberg (see e.g. Foucault 1984a; 1984b; 1984c; 1984e; see also Ashe 1999).

Stoltenberg is also involved in an interrogation of norms and morality across the terrain of men's identities, but he breaks with post-structuralist forms of analysis because he seeks to constitute new ethical normative frameworks for men that oppose the existing norms of men's identities. Post-structuralists have been concerned that if social movements replace one set of regulatory norms with another set, these movements may instantiate new regulatory discourses around identities (Butler 1990). Subsequently, some post-structuralist theorists have tried to avoid developing new ethical frameworks often preferring exclusively deconstructive strategies (see Butler 1990). Stoltenberg in contrast insists on the need for a reconstructive politics of gender that develops normative guidelines for subjects constituted as men. In his own work Stoltenberg develops an ethical framework for men who are prepared to refuse manhood.

Stoltenberg (2000) also shifts from post-structuralism in terms of implementing the ideal of an 'authentic selfhood', which he contrasts with what he calls the 'manhood self'. While the 'manhood self' is orientated towards the oppression of others, the 'authentic self' is orientated towards justice and equality. Stoltenberg contends that the 'authentic self' is buried under the corrupt ethics of sexual difference. The 'authentic self' can be freed from oppressive gender behaviour, he maintains, through a commitment by men to an ethics of gender equity and justice. Therefore Stoltenberg, is proscriptive and suggests that a better self is possible if men follow a new feminist inspired set of ethical practices and guidelines and refuse traditional patriarchal models of gender identity.

Overall Stoltenberg's aim is to harness the indeterminacy of subjectivity to develop new ethical practices on the terrain of gender and sexuality. He therefore fuses a radical construction theory of subjectivity with a set of foundational norms for profeminist men to follow. This fusion enables Stoltenberg to link the deconstruction of the subject to the reconstruction of subjectivity. In this respect Stoltenberg deploys the familiar NSM strategy of working across the terrain of subjectivity to challenge the 'governance' of identity by forms of power, and engages in reconstituting new forms of self-governance for subjects involved in a critical questioning of their identities (see Buechler 2000).

Knowledge, politics and experience

Stoltenberg (1990; 2000) draws on the work of specific radical feminist writers to critically interrogate men's gendered behaviour and the structural forms of power that underpin masculinity. He focuses on the oppressive aspects of masculinity, especially in the arena of sexuality and the body. In particular, he targets men's sexual objectification of women in heterosexual relationships and its representation in pornography. Stoltenberg (1990) claims that men's identity is based around a 'rapist ethics'. Traditional masculinity, for Stoltenberg, is based on the sexual objectification of women and the control of women's bodies. Men's power over women in the arena of sexuality mirrors men's power in the public domain where masculine ethics of aggression, control and the subjection are dominant and are exercised by men over women.

Stoltenberg therefore remains close to certain radical feminist standpoints on gender oppression and sees traditional masculinity as an identity involved in the reproduction of gender oppression and therefore corrupt. As subsequent chapters will expose, the use of radical feminist frameworks by profeminists has been criticised for developing a politics of male guilt. Although, as Goldrick-Jones (2002) notes, there is little evidence of guilt in Stoltenberg's work. In most respects Stoltenberg is a powerful, confident writer who forcefully argues that men can change and develops practical forms of knowledge through which new practices of the subject can be developed. By doing so, Stoltenberg shifts from aspects of the radical feminist paradigm in significant ways.

Stoltenberg (2000) analyses a range of interpersonal relationships in the arena of gender relationships. He examines men's relationship with women and other men, including fathers. This dimension of his engagement with the constitution of men's identities means that Stoltenberg moves beyond particular radical feminist accounts to focus on men's experiences and the processes through which they can be reinterpreted by men and modified in feminist ways. Too often writers neglect this aspect of his theory preferring to examine the implications of his relationship with radical feminist standpoints and his anti-pornography stance (Clatterbaugh 1990; Messner 1997). Certainly Stoltenberg's commitment to the politics of anti-pornography are an important point for analysis in his work and will be discussed below. However, reducing the analysis of Stoltenberg's work on men's identities to his views on pornography and men's sexuality neglects much of his examination of men's identities.

Exposing his development of particular radical feminist perspectives on to the arena of the reconstitution of men's identities, in *The End of Manhood*, Stoltenberg examines the dynamics of masculinities across the personal and private terrains of the family and sexuality and develops a set of reflective practices for men that he believes will allow them to change these practices. His (2000: 46–76) analysis of fatherhood is one of the most insightful of the relationship between sons and fathers in profeminist literature. To engage with the issue of their relationship to their fathers Stoltenberg draws as much on men's experiences as he does on feminist frameworks. He (2000: 64) employs the strategy of critically interrogating men's experiences of their fathers and calls on men to use their memories of their fathers, read through feminism, to consider their familial relationships.

Interrogating men's experience is therefore a central aspect of Stoltenberg's development of self-fashioning practices for men who are engaged in developing profeminist subject positions. For example, Stoltenberg interrogates the experience of feeling that a father is ashamed of his son and reads it through a critical gendered lens that scrutinises the effects of discourses and practices of masculinity in everyday interactions and emotional states. Stoltenberg (2000: 65) records how fathers may feel ashamed of their sons because they were not 'athletic, courageous or well muscled and co-ordinated'. In this respect he strives to expose the gendered networks of identity production that underlie this experience of fathers. He writes:

> your father–realistically and anticipating other men's condemnation–may have feared to be without a mask of manhood himself. And consequently he may have dreaded or loathed the sight of you without yours. You may or may have not been witness to your father's intimidation by other men, how that intimidation was formed in his biography, what shape it took in his daily life. You may only have been the recipient of his gender anxiety when he let you know you where less than nobody to him unless you had your manhood mask in place.
>
> (2000: 64)

Rather than seeing this kind of behaviour as intrinsic to men's identities, Stoltenberg believes that these practices can be changed if men refuse the traditional practices and ethics of manhood. New subjectivities for Stoltenberg emerge from an ethics of justice that involves recognising the rights of others to personhood, equal treatment and liberty from the oppressive effects of masculinity. At the personal level this involves men committing to change and refusing the ideal of men's identity as determined by factors outside of culture. At the personal level Stoltenberg sees the role of the profeminist man as exposing male practices of oppression, challenging other men for their behaviour and arguing for a rejection of traditional masculinity.

Stoltenberg therefore provides a clear indication of how men's experiences can be used as the analytical material that provides critical knowledges around men's identities. He exposes how experience can be interpreted through different standpoints to engender different ethical readings of those experiences and their relationship to networks of gender power. This political reading of men's experience promotes a personal politics by men to change their ethical systems and the material practices that engender their experiences. In this model of politics facets of identity such as bodies, subjectivity and interpersonal communication are involved in the practice of critically interrogating masculinities and the constitution of non-patriarchal practices.

Stoltenberg adopts a similar strategy in relation to men's sexualities. However his reading of sexuality is more firmly located in a radical feminist anti-pornography discourse. Stoltenberg criticises aspects of men's sexuality for objectifying women, however unlike some aspects of the radical feminist analysis of men's sexuality he forcefully argues that these practices and the feelings that they engender are malleable and open to change (see Echols 1989). He (2000: 223) writes: 'sexual feelings are not intrinsically in either selfhood mode or manhood mode'. He believes that sexual practices can move beyond the confines of culturally produced models of heterosexual sexuality.

In Stoltenberg's formulation of profeminist politics, personal change is not enough to develop gender justice. Personal behaviour, while viewed by Stoltenberg as an arena of change, is not the only terrain of power. He maintains that challenging and targeting macro-level power and public conscience must also be part of profeminist politics. As he feels that pornography is a major public issue connected to men's sexualities, he argues that it is important that men campaign publicly on issues of gender inequality and he criticises men who have turned towards an exclusively personal politics. He asks:

> Can a man have a feminist conscience if he does not consistently act on it? . . . Many men of conscience will do little or nothing [in the next decade] . . . they will prefer to discuss their feelings . . . will do only that which makes them feel better about themselves . . . Many men of conscience if they notice that they are doing nothing, will want to spend hours and hours discussing their inertia.
>
> (1990: 60)

Stoltenberg is not against therapy per se and there are therapeutic aspects in his discourse of reinventing men's identities (see 2000). However he does not see therapy as a discourse that will facilitate broad social change. Instead, he believes that the key to changing masculinity lies in the exposure of men's participation in practices of oppression against women and he calls on men to actively reject these practices at the private and public level. Stoltenberg therefore fuses the public, the private and political activism in his model of profeminism, and by doing this he avoids the charge that identity politics can become organised around introspective forms of self-analysis. Furthermore by interweaving his analysis of masculinity with radical feminist perspectives, Stoltenberg blends feminist and profeminist perspectives. Stoltenberg's formulation of profeminism means that there is less organisational and epistemological autonomy in his particular model of profeminism compared with models of profeminism explored in the next chapter. Consequently, feminists have not questioned Stoltenberg's activism to the same extent as, for example, the WRC.

Stoltenberg forsakes the imaginary ontological securities of men's traditional identities and locates those identities on the terrain of critique, deconstruction, and political and ethical struggle. He deploys the idea of mobile and shifting subjectivities in his theory of subjectivity and develops new practices of the self through a critical discourse of gender. However Stoltenberg's particular forging of this strategy of interrogation across the field of identity, which as stated above is common in NSMs, has been criticised by a number of other profeminists. The next section details these criticisms. It also explores Stoltenberg's formulation of the central and often problematic concepts that NSM politics operates around as discussed in Chapter 4, namely identity, the personal and the epistemological foundations of agenda building.

Stoltenberg in the context of profeminism

Not all criticisms that have been made of Stoltenberg's approach to profeminism are persuasive. Clatterbaugh (1990: 53) states that developing a profeminism that uses the radical feminist standpoint on gender creates a problem for coalitions with feminists as radical feminists place a premium on women only spaces and men 'cannot occupy' these spaces. Furthermore, he suggests that given the radical feminist analysis of masculinity as an identity involved in the reproduction of gender power, men who align with some radical feminist perspectives have had difficulty trusting themselves to reform their identities.

Stoltenberg seems to have been able to find a pathway through both difficulties. His work on moving beyond traditional men's identities is both confident and humorous. This confidence pertains not only to his use of radical feminist ideas but also applies to his development of a profeminist analysis of changing men's identities through an engagement with experiences and practices of self-fashioning, which, as indicated above, breaks away from certain aspects of some radical feminist analyses of men's identities. This point will be discussed further below. It can also be noted that Stoltenberg lived with Dworkin thereby 'occupying' the same intimate domestic space as a well known radical feminist.

More pointedly, Stoltenberg has been accused of developing a negative representation of men as 'simply' oppressors and consequently of generating a form of profeminist politics that is based on anger towards men. Stoltenberg certainly highlights issues of men's relationship to 'rapist ethics' as the defining feature of men's sexualities and tends towards an exposure of men's oppressive activities.

Seidler (1997) argues that the kind of attack that radical feminist writers such as Stoltenberg wage on men's identities fills men with feelings of contempt and self-hatred. Seidler advocates a model of profeminism that treats men in a more positive way. His alternative model of profeminism is examined in the next chapter which exposes more clearly the fault lines that have emerged in profeminism around the issue of 'male positivism'. It is important at this point to note in relation to this kind of criticism that Stoltenberg does not develop a model of profeminism that is anti-men in the fashion that critics suggest. He shifts from the kind of negative portrayals of men as inherently nasty that characterised some radical feminist accounts of gender.

This is evident if we compare Stoltenberg's discourse on men with the radical feminist writer Mary Daly's musings on men's subjectivities (2000: xiv-xv: for commentary on alternative standpoints in radical feminism see Grant 1993). Daly's (1979: 53) description of men's identities includes: 'males do indeed identify with "unwanted foetal tissue", for they sense as their own condition the role of controller, possessor, inhabitor of woman. Draining female energy, they *feel* foetal'.

At another point in her analysis Daly calls the figureheads of 'male' power to account as follows:

- Larry Flint, figurehead for the pornographers
- Jack the Ripper, figurehead for serial killers ...
- Sigmund Freud, figurehead for all professional mind-fuckers ...
- His nothingness of Rome and His arrogance, Cardinal Flaw, figureheads for soul killers of women

(quoted in Rowland and Klein 1996: 552)

In contrast Stoltenberg writes:

> History gives us stories of many exceptional humans who were raised to be a man and who exhibited exemplary practical courage. We need not look to myths or fairy tales or make anything up. You may already personally know some historical or contemporary models of such practical courage. You may in your lifetime, personally become one as well.
>
> (2000: 151)

However, the central problem that critics face in claiming that Stoltenberg develops an anti-male discourse is that Stoltenberg does not believe that men exist as an ontological entity. To argue that Stoltenberg is anti-men sidesteps the actual terms of his analysis. Stoltenberg does not criticise men as a pre-discursive category but locates his critique on the terrain of practices reiterated by those people that society has constituted as men within particular material, ethical and moral frameworks. To charge that Stoltenberg is in some sense against men as a category, neglects Stoltenberg's insistence that neither men nor masculinity exist outside of socially constituted gendered subjectivities and practices.

Deploying this theory of subjectivity, he tries to forge a political subjectivity for men that is resistant to many of the normalising discourses and practices of gender. In this respect he works with a theory of the relationship between the subject and political engagement that views the subject as a product of political practices, namely patriarchal practices or anti-patriarchal practices. Therefore the issues that arise from Stoltenberg's analysis of masculinities do not arise from a theory of men's identities as some kind of given, stable identity that is inherently 'bad', but lie in how he formulates his reading of the constitution of men's identities and practices within networks of gender power. This aspect of his analysis of men's gender identities is discussed below.

Writers have also been concerned that the degree of critique that Stoltenberg directs at men, which of course is, in effect, directed at certain practices engaged in by men, creates problems for encouraging men to join the profeminist cause. Messner (1997: 54) quotes Connell, who queries the effect of intensely critical representations of men's subjectivity on profeminist politics when he asks: 'How can a politics whose main theme is anger towards men serve to mobilise men?' As discussed in the next chapter Seidler (1997) argues that the alternative to a very critical analysis of men's practices is a form of profeminist politics that understands the difficulties that men face in reconstituting their identities and the problems they face in terms of the guilt that feminism makes men feel.

The differences between Stoltenberg and Seidler, in terms of the degree of critical engagement with men's identities that they believe profeminism should be involved in, relates to how each writer constitutes the 'we' of profeminist politics. Stoltenberg establishes the 'we' of profeminist politics with reference to concepts such as equality and justice. Participation in the profeminist community therefore requires more than being socially constituted as a man and having concerns about that identity. It demands a clear commitment to a set of political ideals.

As Chapter 8 will explore further, Seidler in contrast constitutes a 'we' in relation to the category of men and men's shared experiences in a culture that has been affected by feminism. Therefore, as the next chapter illustrates, Seidler pushes profeminism towards an analysis of men's experiences amidst dislocating cultural forces and does not develop clear political commitments. As the analysis of Seidler's writings in the next chapter will demonstrate, he develops a model of profeminism that explores men's post-feminist experiences with limited reference to broader gendered inequalities. As suggested in Chapter 4, explorative, introspective explorations of gender are not inherently apolitical. However Seidler increases the possibility of locating profeminist practices within a discursive space that separates it off from the broader political concerns of gender justice, by pushing profeminist explorations of identity towards concerns about the impact of the destabilising effects of gender critique on men. This orientation towards men's identities means that men's experiences/identity become the foundational point for profeminist politics not feminist political principles, as the next chapter will expose more clearly.

Stoltenberg in contrast forges collective identity around a political commitment to gender justice, and deploys men's experiences as a medium for refining and achieving this goal. This approach means that formulations of profeminist practice do not massage away the critical oppositional aspects of the movement in the interests of developing 'softer' approaches to men's practices, in the hope of building a broader profeminist movement.

Maintaining a critical approach to men's identities and the forms of gender inequalities that these identities are linked to, in order to pursue ideals of gender justice, may mean that fewer men are attracted to profeminism. However it ensures that the interrogatory practices of *feminist* gender analysis do not 'fall out of the window' in profeminism and prevents profeminism from moving towards introspective explorations of men's interpretations of their identities that displace the relationship between men's identities/experiences and feminist ideals of gender justice.

This kind of critical approach to developing profeminist politics also increases the likelihood that profeminism maintains a broader relationship with other communities engaged in political interrogations of a range of inequalities across the terrain of multiple and blended identities. A profeminism that ties men's identity to issues of power and democratic forms of justice and equality will have more affinities with other oppositional gendered communities than a profeminism that engages in an introspective analysis of men's subjectivities removed from the concerns of broader social change. Connell (Chapter 10) develops a model of profeminist politics that tries to connect and harness profeminism to this broader arena of democratic struggles across different identity categories that have overlapping political ideals and concerns.

However, Stoltenberg's work exposes how the formulation of movement principles can operate to 'seal' the ethical principles of profeminism, which subsequently creates difficulties in terms of addressing the concerns of other political and subjugated communities. Stoltenberg formulates the ethical and political principles of profeminism through an analysis of the field of power that constitutes men's identities rather than through an analysis of men as a pre-discursive identity. The principles and ethical guides that Stoltenberg formulates for men are condensed in his ideal of an 'authentic self'. By examining Stoltenberg's analysis of the field of gender power across the terrain of men's sexuality, it becomes clear that the construction of an authentic identity for men is based around an analysis of power that refuses the need for 'active listening' to other perspectives that also oppose gender power. It also exposes the problems that Stoltenberg's lack of provisionality around ethics creates in his model of profeminism.

Knowledge, power and resistance

Stoltenberg shapes his ethical principles and notion of an 'authentic self' through a narrow interpretation of men's sexual experiences, explorations and practices. Following certain radical feminist analyses of the relationship between pornography and men's sexuality, Stoltenberg argues that, to develop the 'authentic self', men must reject pornography as it is fundamentally oppressive in its gendered effects. By doing this, he neglects the complex network of power relationships that constitute normative gender subjects and also oppositional gendered subjects. Subjects are located differently within the field of power relationships and this means that different subject positions will emerge across the field of oppositional gender/sexual politics (Butler 1990).

Tucker (1991) takes Stoltenberg to task for not recognising the subversive aspects of gay porn and for neglecting the power dynamics that surround gay sexuality and the experiences of many gay men.

The problem then is that Stoltenberg does not relate his notion of an authentic self to the complex cultural networks of identity constitution that make any final ethical standpoint problematic, especially if that standpoint excludes the experiences, interpretations and political standpoints of other gendered communities. This kind of exclusionary move means that his analysis of the power relationships that constitute gendered identities is partial.

The effect of Stoltenberg's shift from the complex field of gender politics means that Stoltenberg is not able to integrate or recognise practices that lie outside of his ideal of an 'authentic self' but may be radical and resistant to gender power because of their positioning in the gender order. Furthermore by arguing that all men have an undifferentiated relationship to pornography Stoltenberg cannot recognise and refuses 'to adopt (even tentatively) the different standpoints of oppressed groups of men and put them into play with feminist standpoints' (Messner 1997: 55).

Stoltenberg's inattention to the perspectives of other gendered communities means that he is also inattentive to the different modalities of power that cut across men's identities. This inattention to the complexity of the relationship between power and subjectivity means that the 'authentic self' and ethics of justice that Stoltenberg constitutes for men tends to sideline issues of race, class and, as we have seen, sexuality. Stoltenberg's notion of authentic identity and his moral certainty displaces issues of specificity and difference.

Stoltenberg's model of profeminism exposes the problems of categorical essentialism in NSMs that organise around identities (see Chapter 10). This refers to the tendency for identity groups to define identity and its relationship to power in a unitary fashion which suggests that all subjects within that category have the same perspectives, interests and needs (see Butler 1990 on this point). It also exposes the problems of proscriptive politics in NSMs. If social movements establish ethical and political principles as absolute, when searching for alternatives to the status quo of identity constitution, they run the risk of setting up new exclusionary and regulatory structures around the reconstitution of identity that they invoke. Consequently, it seems important for movements to constantly question the foundational principles through which they formulate their ethical frameworks. Ethics perhaps is better viewed as an ongoing process rather than a final achievement for the movement.

Attention to difference and alternative oppositional perspectives does not mean that the 'dream of a common language' will become a reality in profeminism anymore than it has in feminism (Rich 1978).

Different political positions will always be adopted by activists in identity movements, and consensus will not emerge on several issues within movements. Disagreement over values and principles characterise contemporary social movements and these movements, as indicated in Chapter 4, are prone to fragmentation over issues concerning the agendas and principles of movements. Hence Stoltenberg left NOMAS because *Brother* included an article by a gay man that relayed and discussed a sexual relationship he had as a young adult with a minor. The same edition of *Brother* also included an advertisement for an organisation that advocated sex between 'consenting' adults and minors (see Parish 1992 for commentary on this event).

None of the above issues prevent Stoltenberg from engagement in feminist politics; he has drawn out a specific and oppositional standpoint within feminism. Given the myriad forms of feminist democratic practice, there are a number of points of entry for men, and anti-pornography politics represents one of these points. It can too be noted that feminism as a diverse community of contention and dialogue has put divisive standpoints about sexuality into play in gendered politics. Stoltenberg therefore positions himself ethically on an established, and important field of political debate around sexuality, representation and censorship. Stoltenberg's anti-pornography is of course open to the same critiques that have been directed at feminist women who adopt this standpoint (Echols 1989).

Stoltenberg's model of profeminist politics illustrates how profeminism can develop forms of critical practice for men across their identities. It exposes how the personal and political can become fused in profeminism and highlights the way that a community of profeminist men can be forged through political ideals rather than with reference to introspective forms of self-analysis removed from broader issues of justice. However Stoltenberg's model of profeminism exposes the problems involved in building an ethical and political agenda for a movement. This chapter has suggested that attention to difference and the partiality of ethical standpoints are as important in profeminist politics as they are in other movements. The next chapter explores a very different model of profeminist politics through an examination of the work of Seidler. Exploring Seidler's model of profeminism facilitates an engagement with more therapeutic approaches in profeminism, and exposes the kind of issues that emerge in practices of self-introspection by profeminist men, issues that have been touched on in this chapter.

8 Victor J. Seidler

Pain and politics

> It is not shameful to carry the hurts from the past; rather, if we are to revision our different masculinities, an important first step is to find the courage to share more of what we have silently carried inside us for so long.
>
> Victor Seidler (1997: 77)

Victor Seidler was one of the founding members of the Achilles Heel Collective. This group organised to explore men's experiences, power and standpoints in relation to feminism. Achilles Heel supported a plurality of profeminist perspectives (see Rowan 2006 for commentary). Seidler's model of profeminism therefore does not reflect the perspective of all the members of the Collective. His analysis of masculinities and standpoint on profeminist politics did, however, inform some of the themes and debates that emerged in Achilles Heel (see Seidler 1991b).

Seidler's (e.g. 1991a; 1993; 1997) academic work on men's identities is a mix of historical analysis and humanist social philosophy. The main focus of his explorations of the concept of masculinities is on the relationship between the emotional aspects of men's 'inner lives' and the implications of this dimension of men's identities for gender politics. He (especially 1991a; 1997) rejects the model of profeminist politics articulated by Stoltenberg and tries to develop forms of gender politics for men that are less critical of men and more autonomous from the feminist movement. His aim is to develop a form of profeminism that allows men to explore their subjective experiences as gendered subjects beyond the confines of the normative ideals of masculinities and feminist theory.

Masculinity, crisis and wounding

Seidler, like other profeminists, views gender as socially constituted, and he analyses the constitution of men's identities in western societies. His main concerns have been to expose how contemporary men's identities have been affected by a 'Protestant moral culture' and the discourses of the Enlightenment. Seidler (1993) argues that the Enlightenment set up a model of knowledge based around a theory of rational thought that constituted the sensations of the body, human emotions and feelings as extra-rational arenas. Echoing the feminist (e.g. Pateman 1988) critique of Enlightenment thinkers, Seidler (1994) argues that the Enlightenment theory of rationality was highly gendered. Philosophers such as Kant associated reason and rationality with men, and emotion and irrationality with women.

While feminists (e.g. Lloyd 1984) have examined how the Enlightenment ideal of reason operated as a form of phallocentric thought that supported gender inequities, Seidler (1993) has been more concerned to map the impact of Enlightenment models of human reason on the cultural ideals of manliness. Seidler argues that contemporary men continue to associate normative masculinity with a form of rationality that requires the suppression of the emotional aspects of subjectivity. Consequently men repress their feelings. This suppression of men's feelings is further encouraged by the existence of, what Seidler (1989; 1993; 1997) calls, 'the Protestant culture of guilt' emanating from Calvinism. He contends that this culture operates around ideas that desire and feelings are inherently evil and must be suppressed. Consequently men, he claims, feel guilt and inadequacy when they express their emotions. Commenting on the effect of Protestant ideologies on men's sexualities, Seidler writes:

> within a Protestant moral culture we have grown up feeling guilty about our sexual fantasies because we assume they indicate our evil natures. So we learn to suppress our fantasies and feel ashamed ... There is no sense, within a Protestant moral culture, that we might be able to act them out and explore the meanings that they hold.
>
> (1997: 16)

Seidler argues that hegemonic 'male' identity, with its emphasis on the denial of emotions, has a number of negative consequences for men. He suggests that men's emotional suppression creates difficulties in interpersonal relationships and causes men emotional pain that they cannot express, because the dominant models of masculinity prohibit such practices. Seidler, like Bly, argues that men suffer emotional wounds because of society's structuring of men's identities. His (1997) work documents men's emotional pain caused by distance fathers, childhood experiences and the difficulties of expressing feelings from a masculine subject position.

Recognising how men's social role causes men to suppress their emotions and feelings is important for men, according to Seidler. He contends that expressing emotion allows men to connect to an aspect of their subjectivity that traditional models of masculinity have denied them and also enables them to deal with the emotional wounds and pain that men's identities create. He argues that because Bly recognises men's wounds he has been able to 'speak to the heart and soul of men that have been starved of recognition and nourishment' (1997: 38). Dealing with the emotional aspects of men's identities for Seidler, also provides a basis for reformulations of men's identities. He maintains that exploring men's 'inner lives' can help men connect to women and children in less patriarchal ways. Seidler's model of reforming men's identities will be discussed further below.

While Seidler (1997) echoes Bly's claims that men are wounded though their experiences as men, he differentiates his theory of masculinity from Bly's model. He rejects Bly's essentialism, and argues that the model of the wild man in Bly's writings could quite easily be interpreted by some men as an invitation to return to a macho, aggressive form of manhood. Seidler also refuses Bly's Jungian theory of archetypal subjectivity (see Rowan 1987 for an alternative Jungian framework). He (1993; 1997) argues that in order to understand their masculinities men need to engage in a historical analysis that examines how men's identities have been socially constituted. Furthermore as discussed above, he believes that men's inner lives need to be explored, and maintains that practices that explore men's emotions can be harnessed to reconstituting men's identities in more positive ways.

While Seidler rejects Bly's general analytical framework, he does develop some points of agreement with Bly, especially in relation to the impact of feminism on modern men. Echoing some of Bly's concerns about feminism's influence on how men perceive their identities, Seidler argues that profeminist politics must maintain a degree of autonomy from the feminist analysis of masculinities. With his emphasis on men's emotions and his concern that profeminists maintain some political distance from feminism, Seidler develops a model of profeminist politics that rejects many aspects of Stoltenberg's profeminist practices.

Changing men's identities

Seidler (1997: 14) argues that to understand men's pain, 'we have to be ready to challenge feminist notions that would identify masculinity exclusively as a relationship of power'. Seidler shifts from critical feminist investigations of men's identities that chart the costs of masculinities for women, towards an analysis of men's lives and experiences. He believes that this kind of analysis has become very important for men who want to reform their identities in profeminist ways. Feminism, he claims, has been too critical of men. Seidler (e.g. 1989) accepts the feminist claim that men and women are in a relationship of inequality and acknowledges that society is structured around a value system that benefits men. He (1997) also concords with Bly that feminism as a social movement has been positive for women. However, like Bly, he maintains that feminism has created difficulties for men.

As outlined above, Seidler maintains that hegemonic forms of men's identities wound men. He claims that feminism has wounded men further by labelling them oppressors. He suggests that men who adopt critical feminist interpretations of men's experiences may be engendering feelings of self-hatred and guilt for men. Seidler claims that building profeminism around a negative interpretation of masculinity is not the best approach for profeminists because this wounds men further. He argues that a politics of guilt emerges out of this wounding and claims that guilt and negativity about men does not produce an effective form of profeminist politics, but is instead potentially debilitating for men (1997: 6). He believes that men should not fall into the trap of blaming themselves for women's oppression. Instead, he believes that men who wish to change their identity in a progressive way need to deal with the hurt that feminist discourse creates for men. Seidler argues that what feminism and profeminist men need to do is address the issue of men's identities in a less critical fashion. Rather than criticising men, Seidler believes that men should be given the opportunity to talk about their emotional hurt, and their insecurities as men. Furthermore he claims that negativity about men has implications for the expansion of profeminism. He argues that profeminism cannot reach out to other men if it remains with the framework of criticising men for being men.

Moreover Seidler criticises writers such as John Stoltenberg who argue that men should reject their masculinity. Again, according to Seidler, this kind of negative view of men reinforces cultural ideas about masculinity already prevalent in culture. Seidler argues that men need to be 'male affirmative', not ashamed or guilt ridden. He suggests that 'male baiting' arises from too close an alignment by men with feminism. Writers such as Stoltenberg who adopt a radical feminist analysis are viewed by Seidler as supporting and reinforcing feminism's negative discourse on men's identity. For Seidler, this is why feminism is not always a resource for men who want to change their subjectivities.

Given his views on contemporary masculinity and the impact of feminism on men, Seidler does not celebrate the crisis of masculinity unlike some other contributors to *Achilles Heel* magazine. For example the Jungian analyst, Samuels (1995), sees the crisis of masculinity as a positive development and argues that men should embrace the contemporary disruption around their identities. He argues that men have been afflicted by 'gender certitude' and maintains that the confusion that surrounds masculinity is cause for 'celebration' as it opens a space for men to explore new possibilities and identities. In Seidler's (1997) view men should not celebrate the so-called crisis of masculinity. He argues that men need to explore the difficulties that the crisis surrounding men's identities has created for contemporary men.

Seidler shifts (especially 1997) profeminism towards a therapeutic model of identity exploration that helps men express how they feel about their lives as men, the impact of feminism and the contemporary confusion that surrounds their identities. Seidler (1997) gives some examples of this kind of exploration. He provides biographical details of his difficulties when he was young. His father died when he was still a boy. His mother went out to work and he felt that he had to support her and suppress his own feelings to avoid creating any more strain for her (1997: 70–71). He (1997: 70) relays the story of another man who felt deep emotional hurt when, at eight years old, his father refused to hold his hand when out walking. Men, according to Seidler, suffer this kind of pain because of the way that masculinity has been socially constituted and have no way of expressing it. This is why, for Seidler, therapy and men's groups' explorations of members' life histories is important; it enables men to deal with their feelings in a supportive environment.

For Seidler the exposure of the emotional aspects of men's identities illustrates why models of profeminist politics such as Stoltenberg's are prone to failure. He (see e.g. 1991a; 1997) continually reinforces the claim throughout his writings on men's identities that men cannot change through a 'sheer act of will'. He (1997: 67) maintains that Freud grasped this problem because he understood that just because 'we learn to hide and conceal our wounds [this] does not mean that they go away, for they still exist as wounds in our inner emotional lives, waiting to be recognised'.

For Seidler self-analysis is important in terms of exploring men's hurt, but he also argues that this process helps men to develop their emotional side and enables them to understand and express their emotional needs. He believes that if men can find a way to develop their emotional potential this will lead to the creation of new subject positions for men no longer based on the suppression of emotional life. For example Seidler (1997) argues that connecting to the emotional aspects of life is important for developing new forms of fatherhood for men. He argues that if men become more involved with children they will develop the capacity to care for others. It is, according to Seidler, only when men have developed the affective aspects of their subjectivity that they will be able to understand the emotional needs of others. He writes:

> Relating to babies can teach us a way of communicating that exists prior to language and so help us touch our own physicality and non-verbal expression . . . As we learn to appreciate the time we spend with young babies and infants it can be a way of accepting love and nourishment that we too easily reject from adults. In its own way it is part of an initiation into manhood, for it potentially awakens us to qualities of care and love that we might not have thought ourselves capable of.
>
> (1997: 110)

Politics, pain and power

Seidler's profeminism is based around personal and group explorations of men's personal identities. Chapter 4 suggested that explorations of identity by identity movement participants means that some groups can act as cultural laboratories that challenge and disrupt normative understandings of specific identities. It suggested that explorations of personal identity may have some critical value for political communities engaged in micro-level and macro-level antagonisms around normative gendered and sexual identities. As Chapter 4 illustrated, studies of other forms of identity politics have exposed that disconnection from public politics does not make more introspective work on identity political redundant. Given this, it seems important to map the kind of interrogation that introspective explorations of identity in this model of profeminism produces and its impact on how profeminist politics is located theoretically and politically.

In some respects Seidler's analysis of men's identity challenges hegemonic formulations of men's identities. Middleton writes that:

> Men in most western cultures are not supposed to show any emotion in public life other than anger, except in certain ritually defined circumstances, because anger is masculine power at its most impressive. Otherwise men should control themselves, and maintain a firm jaw in the face of trouble. Women commonly can show any emotion except anger.
>
> (1992: 212)

As suggested in Chapter 4, the expression of emotion by men challenges the public/private divide and undermines notions that men must not show emotional vulnerability. Middleton (1992: 230) elaborates this point when he claims that: 'Masculinity has a vested interest in blocking unheroic, masculine self-analysis.' Furthermore Seidler locates profeminist practice at the micro-level of intimate personal and bodily practices; an arena that post-structuralist writers such as Butler and Foucault formulate as arenas of power.

However Seidler's particular constitution of practices aimed at supporting emotional exploration by men limit the oppositional potential of incursions into the domain of personal identity and micro-level forms of power. Seidler's demand for profeminist autonomy from feminism means that the problem of experiential exclusivity also emerges in Seidler's model of profeminism. Seidler insulates men's interrogation of their identities from feminist standpoints that articulate women's experiences of men's identities and agency. By pushing feminist analysis out of the arena of profeminist analysis of men's experiences, Seidler reproduces the Enlightenment notion of a self-referential subject that can formulate critical knowledge from its own standpoint (see Ashe 1999).

This problem is exacerbated by the narrowness of Seidler's analysis of men's identities. By concentrating on the emotional aspects of men's lives and the concept of wounded male subjectivity, Seidler excludes many dimensions of critical studies of masculinity by feminists and profeminist writers. Therefore, he contains men's explorations of their identity within a discursive space that places a premium on allowing men to articulate their experiences honestly and openly but does not provide the kind of critical tools that would enable men to interrogate those experiences. More pointedly, his analysis of the constitution of the ideals of manhood through Enlightenment formulations of reason deflects attention from the system of gender relationships that continues to position men within socially dominant positions. Seidler's narrow focus on Enlightenment discourse and 'the Protestant culture of guilt' means that he fails to properly contextualise men's identities within contemporary societies and he also fails to historicise men's identities beyond Enlightenment discourse.

This means that the structural, material and genealogical constitution of men's identities is largely excluded from Seidler's analysis of contemporary masculinities. Other profeminists have outlined some of the effects of Seidler's type of approach to profeminist politics. Messner (1997: 105) has commented that the 'idea that men's "need" to dominate others is the result of an emotional deficit overly psychologizes a reality that is largely structural'. Connell (1995) has also argued that framing men's identities within psychological discourses diverts men's attention from the need for structural changes. McMahon has also criticised Seidler's model of profeminism directly and notes the de-politicising effects of some forms of psychological explanations of men's identities and social positioning. He also argues that Seidler's focus on men's psychology suggests that men are psychologically disadvantaged compared to women. This position, he claims, suggests that men have 'unique' emotional problems. For McMahon (1993: 689) 'such accounts, implicitly or explicitly, construct a female "other" who is not emotionally damaged: her relational potential is intact, her emotional needs are acknowledged'. Seidler's discourse of profeminist politics illustrates how narrow conceptualisations of men's identities produced through discourses of therapy reduce the critical space for interrogations of men's experiences.

A few examples of profeminist explorations of men's identities will illustrate the problems of experiential exclusivity in forms of profeminist explorations of identity guided by notions of 'male positivism' and the need to avoid feeling guilty 'because you are a man'. The examples below also expose the lack of attention to external gendered networks of power in some therapeutic forms of profeminism. These examples illustrate the effects of men's open and honest articulation of their experiences in a context that displaces the critical tools of gender analysis.

Again it is important to note that Achilles Heel supported a range of perspectives on issues relating to men and masculinities. However it is possible to identify how open and 'less critical' discussions within *Achilles Heel* magazine, about men's gender identity and gender relationships, that reflect 'male positivism', often lacked the kind of critical engagement that characterised the contributions of profeminists such as Hearn, to the magazine (see Chapter 9). For example Banks' (1995) article discusses his sexual experiences honestly, openly and within the confines of male positivism. Banks, a psychologist and therapist, exposes how self-analysis of his identity and his experiences allowed him to resolve two difficulties that he was experiencing as a man. Banks discusses his experiences of heterosexual relationships and tells readers that he has a 'fear of fucking'. He details the guilt that he experiences when he enters into a sexual relationship with a woman. For example, he relays how he felt uncomfortable having sex with women because he believed that 'women don't like sex'. Banks does not provide an explanation for his belief about women's sexuality illustrating how he misses an opportunity to critically explore his views as a man in relation to women's sexuality.

Banks' then openly discusses the difficulty he experiences in controlling his penis when he is in intimate situations with women. He regularly visits a masseuse and during one of these visits he has an erection. He (1995) writes: 'The association in my mind was "hard-on = dirty/porn/women-are-sex-objects. If I got a hard-on, didn't that mean ... that effectively I was treating this very nice woman as a prostitute?"' However the masseuse told him that it was 'OK' to have an erection. He writes:

> I can really relate to men who pay women for 'relief', for me to be told that it was OK to have a hard-on while receiving a massage from her was a huge relief ... men who pay for 'relief' are paying a woman to tell them that their fears about sexual feelings, and the sexual feelings themselves, are OK.
>
> (1995)

The article then details his fears when he was experiencing a very intimate moment with his girlfriend. Banks tells the reader that that he wanted intercourse, while he felt that his girlfriend wanted non-sexual intimacy, and he has 'this strong feeling that it is wrong'. He then relays that he met a woman who initiated sex by shouting 'fuck me, fuck me hard'. Due to his experiences with this woman he discovered:

> that sometimes I actually like to fuck aggressively. There is a part of me which feels feelings which I imagine are not that different from what a rapist feels ... if she had told me to stop I would have stopped. That makes it different from rape. But I think the feelings may not be so different.
>
> (1995)

Banks draws a number of conclusions about gender relationships from his analysis of his bodily and sexual experiences with women; he writes: 'the best way for men to help themselves and women is to explore their feelings without judgement. That means creating a space where any and all feelings are acceptable, and can be shared acknowledged and gone into'.

The problem is that Banks' experiences are not 'gone into': they are not interrogated through a critical discourse of gender. His experiences are articulated from his point of view. There is no exploration of why his sexual feelings take a particular form. There is no analysis of the relationship between cultural constitutions of masculinity and his identification with rapists and men who visit prostitutes. There is no analysis of the relationship between his experiences, perceptions and broader structures of power. Overall his discourse seems to be clearly guided by notions that men should not feel guilty and should relay their experiences rather than critically engage with them.

The conclusions he draws from his articulation of his experiences exposes the dangers of experiential exclusivity in profeminist practices of identity interrogation. At the end of the article he gives a lengthy description of what he likes sexually, which he ends by telling readers that his lovers rarely engage enough in satisfying him. Clearly, existing ideas that suggest that men's sexual pleasure is more important than its effects on others, have coloured this man's approach to his sexual experiences. He reinforces traditional ideas about phallic sexuality.

The Achilles Heel Collective (Seidler 1991b) wrote in the 1990s that one of the most important breakthroughs that men in group discussion made was not feeling guilty because you're a man. Feeling guilty and critically interrogating men's identities however are different forms of engagement with identity. The former may or may not encourage people to become engaged in profeminism but the latter builds critical oppositional gendered discourses that can 'feed' movements that want to challenge the system of gendered relationships. As another article from the *Achilles Heel* magazine will illustrate, this kind of critical analysis is absent in some profeminist men's self-interrogations.

Duffell's (1997) article for the *Achilles Heel* magazine brings together aspects of Seidler's model of profeminism. Duffell, a psychotherapist, adopts a 'no blame' discourse of therapy and assumes a 'male positive' orientation. Duffell runs therapy groups for couples. He relays in his article how he employed therapeutic analysis in his own relationship. Three times divorced, he ended his third marriage to have a relationship with his wife at the time of writing. Duffell tells of how the new relationship was full of conflict. One of the major difficulties to emerge was that Duffell's third wife had provided him with sex on demand and he tells readers that she had an orgasm almost instantaneously on the commencement of intercourse. His fourth wife often refused to have sex with him and did not reach orgasm so easily. Due to this conflict, 'desperate' and 'vulnerable', Duffell had an affair. He (1997) states that 'it wasn't until my "sexually acting out" in secret outside the relationship that we got to the bottom of it'.

Duffell does not explain how the couple achieved this insight into the root of their marital 'problems'. After his discussion of the difficulties in his marriage he talks about the therapy groups he runs for couples and declares (1997) that 'women frequently find that to sit in their genuine femininity becomes in fact the opposite of losing power'. In this article Duffell narrates the events in his marriage through a limited and male-centred standpoint. Again he prioritises his sexual needs and does not subject his experiences and agency to critique. In the article his reaction to his wife not meeting his sexual demands is defined as 'normal.' In this case the adoption of a language of therapy frames traditional forms of male infidelity, deceit and disloyalty as reasonable psychological responses to relationship difficulties. He ends by suggesting that passive forms of femininity and women's 'adjustment' in heterosexual contexts will help couples deal with men's infidelity.

The above analysis, however, does not mean that 'blaming and baiting' discourses within profeminism necessarily provide more effective forms of profeminist practices. The idea of profeminists being 'male affirmative' emerged from consciousness-raising groups that were, according to Rowan (1987), 'depressing places.' Given that Rowan's more favoured practice of self-analysis involved hooding men, while other men shouted accusations of sexism at them, it can be suggested that when consciousness-raising is reduced to a critical analysis of men's individual actions it may indeed verge on being 'masochistic' (see Pease 2000 for an alternative description of men's groups).

However as feminist practices of consciousness-raising illustrate people's behaviour is not simply a product of personal agency but an effect of broader social structures and regulatory discourses. Hence, Butler (1990: 10) understands gender as 'a shifting and contextual phenomenon'. For Butler (1990: 10) 'gender does not denote a substantive being, but a relative point of convergence among culturally and historically specific sets of relations.' Moreover a theory of subjectivity as socially produced challenges the dichotomy of 'male positivism' and 'male' baiting. Masculinity is a myth and personal interrogations of identity expose the power effects of that myth; they do not necessarily have to be reduced to the personal, intentional agency of men to produce a discourse of 'blame.' They can instead become a discourse of interrogation across the political, the personal and the material realms of identity constitution.

As both Banks' and Duffell's articles illustrate, men's open and honest articulation of their feelings, experiences and perspectives provides much material for critical analysis. However critical analysis seems to require listening to the perspectives, standpoints and experiential interpretations of other oppositional gendered communities, who are involved in *critically* challenging gendered norms. This kind of attention to other critical communities allows men to locate their perspectives beyond personal, self-referential accounts. Moreover, this kind of approach locates experience in a discursive space that supports intersecting critical discourses that inform and challenge each other. The 'inward gaze' in profeminist politics as Middleton (1992) terms it, benefits from an outward gaze towards the relationship between personal identity and broader networks of power, and the knowledges of other gendered communities.

Such an approach to men's personal experiences of their identities would support a more disruptive gendered analysis of men's pain. Seidler's narrowness of focus and orientation towards the psychological insights of Freud means that the concept of men's pain is formulated without reference to the historical or social context of men's identities. Kimmel (1998: 64) engages in a historical analysis of contemporary men's pain. He writes that men's pain often emerges as men interpret their experiences in relation to an older discourse of men's rights; therefore men's pain is caused by men's power. This kind of analysis does not mean that the concept of men's pain has to be excluded from profeminist engagements, as some feminists have suggested (e.g. hooks 1998). Pain, like experience, can act as the material of political explorations by men around their identities, if the social, historical and political aspects of the concept of pain are recognised in profeminist discourses and practices.

To be fair, as noted earlier, Seidler does try to develop new forms of fatherhood through his analysis of men's suppression of the emotional aspects of life. Seidler does not outline what a reconstituted form of fatherhood entails. He does suggest that reformulated models of fatherhood would, in some way, revolve around increasing men's emotional involved with children. However Seidler's discourse of fatherhood is again limited by the lack of an 'outward gaze'. The following quote illustrates this problem. Based on his own experiences as a father he writes:

> I appreciated the ways that I was bonding with Daniel and the love that flowed so easily and naturally towards him, while knowing that I was not having the same kind of relationship Anna was having through breast feeding. I did not feel jealous ... Somehow I had worked through the idea that having an equal relationship did not mean having the same relationship ... I felt more easy with the idea that at least for a while the primary relationship would be between mother and child and that my role as father was to support this relationship. I was to sustain and protect it, whilst also developing my own relationship with Daniel.
>
> (1997: 106)

Seidler's definition of parental relationships seems on some level to reflect traditional ideas about men's role as protectors of the family. His reference to biology, as the defining feature of men and women's relationship to children, misses the opportunity to explore how the regulatory ideals of gender identities produce particular forms of fatherhood and motherhood. Furthermore, if we look back to Seidler's exploration of fatherhood discussed in the previous section, it is not clear how relating to babies would allow men to experience pre-discursive emotions. As Seidler's own recourse to biology as the defining feature of the father's specific relationship to children exposes, individuals conceive of their relationship to their children in ways that are saturated with traditional ideas about gender identities.

A critical problematisation of parenting would require an examination of the discourses that produce subjects' understanding of parenting and the power-effects of these discourses. Such a problematisation is more probable if profeminism locates its analysis of masculinity in the material and discursive networks of contemporary social systems, instead of shifting it to an ill-defined pre-discursive realm of emotions that sidesteps the importance of these systems.

Chapter 3 suggested that men are produced by gender power. This chapter detailed Butler's (1990) argument that any identification with identity necessarily produces that power through the reproduction of the social matrix of sexual difference. Butler suggests that as long as gendered subjects remain within the intelligibility of the discourse and practices of sexual difference they will reiterate aspects of normative gender identity. However, as identity movements choose to operate through the category of identity, it is important to analyse the degree to which the practices of politics reiterates normative gendered identities and the political effects of that reiteration.

The profeminist discourses examined in this chapter illustrate how practices of resistance to normative identities can reproduce the traditional power-effects of those identities through a discourse of liberation. While subversion of power from within identity, according to Butler, always involves some reproduction of the logic of power that constitutes identities, it is still possible to suggest that the way that identity politics deploys strategies will have different effects on identities. Seidler's profeminism does not develop the kind of subversive strategies that can effectively contest and disrupt men's identities from within the category of men's identities.

It can also be noted that some aspects of Seidler's analysis of men's experiences have tended towards universalising the experiences of white, middle class men in profeminist politics. Seidler at times developed forms of profeminist knowledge and practices by formulating universal categories of men's needs and men's experiences. However Seidler (2006) has recently added a new dimension to his analysis of men and masculinities by examining young men within newly globalised cultures. This broadens Seidler's contextual analysis of men and masculinities. However, the framework that he applies to young men in various geographical contexts reflects his earlier standpoint on the importance of men exploring their feelings, emotions and gender negotiations 'without the moralising that still haunts the tradition of sexual politics' (2006: 14). He (2006: 13) criticises Connell's structuralist analysis of masculinities (Chapter 10) by arguing that perspectives that concentrate on men's power limit the space for young men to discuss their lives. He (2006: 147) argues that such perspectives position men as 'bad' because of the 'power that they can take for granted'. Reiterating the claims of his previous work Seidler (2006: 14) writes: 'As long as we think of masculinities as locked into relations of power with each other, it is difficult to understand how men can change through processes of transforming masculinities in specific cultures, histories and traditions.'

Connell and Hearn, the next two writers examined in this volume, contest the assumptions underlying Seidler's model of profeminist. These theorists have developed theoretical frameworks that interrogate men's personal identities and also macro-level forms of gender power. Each offers an alternative framework for men who want to engage in increasing gender justice at personal and public levels.

9 Jeff Hearn

Men, identity and power

> Men's actions against patriarchies are always problematic, always contradictory, always partial – the prospect of a 'total strategy' is illusory.
>
> Jeff Hearn (1992: 231)

Hearn has been active in a number of profeminist men's groups, including Profeministimiehet. Aside from his activism, Hearn has been a key figure in developing and driving forward the field of profeminist research. His analysis of men and masculinities has been wide ranging, and includes a number of critical studies of men in relation to the arenas of management, organisations, social welfare, reproduction and men's violence (e.g. Hearn, 1983; 1987; Hearn and Parkin 1987; Hearn 1992; 1998a; Hearn and Pringle with members of CROME 2006). Charting and theorising gender power and men's relationships to those networks have been the central planks of Hearn's analysis of various gendered arenas. These critical studies of men, gender and power have helped inform his analysis of the implications of gender power for reconfigurations of men's identities and profeminist strategies.

Hearn's (1983; 1987) early academic interventions traced the relationships between power and knowledge across the terrain of gender to expose how critical forms of social theory, such as Marxism, theorised class inequalities but failed to take proper account of the operation and effects of patriarchal power in the generation of social inequities. Hearn (1987) subsequently reformulated Marxist theories of power to develop a neo-Marxist theory of patriarchy. While Hearn has developed his analysis of men's power beyond neo-Marxism, the concept of gender power has remained central to his analysis of men, profeminist politics and the possibilities of gender transformations (see 1992; 1998a). Hearn's work on organisations has also influenced his focus on the macro and public levels of power (see e.g. Hearn and Parkin 1987; Collinson and Hearn 1996; 2005; Hearn and Parkin 2001).

Highly aware of the relationships between power and knowledge, while sharing concerns with other analysts about the effects of the new interrogatory discourses around the concept of masculinities, Hearn has been at the forefront of investigating the epistemological foundations of studies of men. In response to feminist and profeminist anxieties about the direction of studies on men and masculinities, Hearn co-authored a set of 'baseline' principles for critical studies of men (Hearn *et al.* 1983). He later reiterated and expanded these principles with Morgan (Hearn and Morgan 1990). Hearn (e.g. 1998a; 1998b) has continued to highlight the importance of a critical orientation towards the generation of profeminist knowledges and activism.

Hearn's focus on gender power and his analysis of the constitution of gendered knowledges about men means that he has developed a different model of profeminist politics to Seidler. Hearn's theoretical framework has also meant that he has prioritised a set of analytical issues across the concepts of men, power, knowledge and gender transgression that are less prevalent in Stoltenberg's work. He has therefore, been able to stretch profeminist analysis onto new conceptual terrains.

The rest of this chapter discusses how Hearn's focus on the category of gender power and his attention to epistemological issues in profeminism has enabled him to develop a range of conceptual tools for profeminist analysis, which in turn, broadens profeminism's reflexivity in relation to the movement's political practice across private and public arenas. It also examines how Hearn's general analysis of gender acts to question dimensions of more therapeutic approaches. The next section examines the development and application of the concept of gender power in Hearn's profeminist interventions. Later sections expose how Hearn's theory of gender power guides his analysis of profeminist epistemologies and allows him to reflectively mark arenas for profeminist politics.

Men, masculinity and power

Hearn views men as a socially constituted, multiple and variable social group (see Hearn and Collinson 1994). He subsequently opposes constructions of men as a biologically determined or ontological category. Although Hearn's theorisation of men and masculinities deconstructs formulations of men as ontologically prior to the social constitution of gender, he suggests that, collectively men can still be viewed as representing a gender class.

The concept of gender class emerged in strands of Second Wave feminism. Both its conceptual clarity and usefulness for feminism have been contested (see Lloyd 2005: 55–74). Acknowledging the concerns that have surrounded the theoretical utility of the concept of gender class in feminist analysis, Hearn (e.g. 1987; 1992; 1998a; Hearn and Collinson 1994) deploys the term to capture the effects of the historical and ongoing politically constituted relationships of power between men and women. Hearn (1992) argues that social, economic, symbolic and political structures produce gendered power imbalances. Differentials of power between men and women, Hearn contends, means that men collectively and individually, albeit differentially, benefit most from the social organisation of gender relationships. Hearn therefore argues that gender relations reflect the patriarchal ordering of society.

Hearn is careful to highlight how the advantages that men accrue from gendered networks of power are multifaceted and fragmentary. He (1992) notes, for example, how white, heterosexual men located in higher social strata of society benefit more from established systems of gender power than other groups that face disadvantage or discrimination due to cross-cutting identities such as race, class or sexuality (see also Hearn and Collinson 1994).

However, in terms of the overall system of gender power, Hearn's (1987; 1992) analysis suggests that men, regardless of their social location will benefit, albeit at different points in gender systems, from their identities as men to the detriment of women. Hearn argues that even if men are not directly involved in oppressive practices towards women, the economic and social structuring of gender relationships and social expectations for men operates to men's general advantage. Hearn, therefore, traces differences between men and exposes how those differences interact to create patriarchal relationships and other forms of power (Hearn and Collinson 1994: 115). Based on this analysis, Hearn (1998a: 35) contends that: 'Men are members of a powerful social category that is invested with power. This has the consequence that membership of that group or category brings power, if only by association.'

For Hearn (1987; 1992; 1998a) men's power is supported though economic, political, institutional and discursive structures. Within these frameworks men's agency at the private and public levels of society reproduces the broader material dimensions of men's power.

At the macro-level Hearn has exposed how patriarchal relationships operate through large social institutions and widespread meaning systems that constitute the category of sexual difference. For example Hearn (e.g. 1992) illustrates how men remain dominant in macro-level structures, such as the state. He (e.g. 1983) also exposes the operation of patriarchal agency at the micro-level through men's everyday actions which reproduce gendered inequalities of power in private arenas such as the family.

Men are bound together in Hearn's analysis as a distinctive class because of their relationships to patriarchal power. As a later section will illustrate, the notion of gender class in Hearn's work is not fixed and is constantly deconstructed as he exposes the complexities of gender relationships particularly through his emphasis on the importance of mapping men's different social locations within patriarchal systems. Reflecting the provisional status of theorisations of men as a coherent category or class, Hearn (1998a: 4) comments: 'It is very important to acknowledge the interplay of these unities and differences between men; the paradox of the recognition of men as a gender class and the deconstruction of the monolith of men.'

In Hearn's work on masculinities the concepts of gender class and patriarchy operate to expose how men become centred as a category. Charting how men become constituted as a certain kind of social category is a necessary political and theoretical move because 'an emphasis on the specificities [of masculinities] can degenerate to a diversified pluralism with insufficient attention to structures of power and oppression' (Hearn and Collinson 1994: 113). Hearn (1998a) instantiates the concepts of patriarchy and gender class in his analysis of gender to 'name' the category of men so as to constantly de-centre this concept by exposing the complexities that destabilise the 'neat' gendered binaries that they produce.

While the category of gender class remains unstable in Hearn's work, his claim that men share some beneficial relationship to systems of gender power allows him to position issues of power at the forefront of his analysis of contemporary masculinities. More generally he has argued that profeminist theory and political practice need to be guided by attention to men's relationships to power (e.g. 1983; 1992; 1998a; 1998b). For Hearn (1998a: 4) mapping power is not only important for examinations of men as a collective, but is also important in terms of examining men's individual identity because 'the psychological and social identity called "man" says and shows power relationships'.

Hearn's (e.g. 1983; 1987; 1992; 1998a) academic agenda has exposed how men exercise and benefit from gender power in their relationships with women. Consequently his political agenda has operated around the development of strategies that involve men in oppositional gendered struggles that challenge the gender structuring of social institutions, deconstruct the normative discourses of gender, and reconstitute men's individual behaviour and identity in profeminist directions (see for e.g. 1983; 1992; 1998a; 1998b; 1999).

Hearn's theoretical and political differences to Seidler are clearly evident. As discussed below, Hearn's prioritisation of the category of power in profeminist theory and practice means that he develops a model of profeminism that ties it closely to feminist standpoints and politics, is critical of men, and works towards the transformation of differentials of power between men and women. Furthermore, Hearn's theorisation of the concepts of men's identity, experience, knowledge, public and private contrasts sharply with Seidler's articulation of these concepts to produce an alternative analytical framework for profeminism. The next two sections of this chapter explore how Hearn pushes profeminist theory and practice beyond the limitations of 'male-positive' approaches.

Hearn's focus on men's power means that, while he employs a different theoretical analysis of power, his interrogation of men and masculinities has some affinities with Stoltenberg's standpoint. Hearn and Stoltenberg certainly share a common concern that profeminism should challenge men's power. However their work exhibits clear differences in terms of their approach to power, identity and politics. Stoltenberg's grounding of profeminist resistance in an authentic, and by implication, pre-political self means that he does not consider the political 'locatedness' of profeminist activity as thoroughly as does Hearn. Hearn's tendency to continually rethink and re-theorise power, politics and resistance across the terrain of men and masculinities means that he is more aware that profeminist subject positions cannot simply reject power but are constituted through existing networks of power. Hearn's consideration of profeminist practices as political practices submerged in power relationships, means that he places a range of important issues on the profeminist agenda: issues that will be discussed below.

To expand on these aspects of Hearn's contribution to the development of profeminist theorising and agendas, the next section outlines his analysis of men's development of knowledge around masculinities. This section also outlines the model of critical studies on men that emerged from Hearn's and other writers' reflections on men's analyses of their gendered identities, including the development of critical autobiography (e.g. Hearn 2005). Rather than approach the development of critical studies on men chronologically, the next section considers how Hearn's exploration of knowledges about men exposes the potential power-effects of those knowledges on gendered power relationships.

Knowledge, power and politics

Hearn (1998b) recognises that studies of men are not new. As men have traditionally been the dominant gender, studies of human societies have often translated into studies of men. Hearn argues that social scientists have continually studied the organisation of society by exploring men and men's agency. These studies of society usually produce knowledges about men but do not recognise men as gendered subjects. Hearn (1998b: 788) writes that men are either absent from the analysis, referred to but not interrogated, or are recognised as having a dominant social position but take men's social dominance for granted. Subsequently 'malestream' social science has tended to present a non-gendered analysis of men (786).

Hearn (1998b: 786) argues that 'not naming men as men, is a structured way of not beginning to talk of and question men's power in relation to women, children, young people, and indeed other men'. Hearn notes how this traditional approach to thinking about men has been challenged by new discourses that explicitly examine men as gendered subjects. However the explicit analysis of men, he argues, does not necessarily lead to oppositional gendered knowledges. Therefore Hearn maintains that it is important to recognise the social basis of knowledge production when examining the generation of knowledges about men. Hearn (1998b: 807) writes: 'What is called social theory cannot be isolated from the social relations of knowledge.' Hearn also stresses the importance of a historical approach in examinations of the interconnections between knowledges about men and masculinities and power. Hearn's recognition that academic knowledges about men shift historically and emerge from within existing relations of gender power can also be applied to discourses about men's gendered identities generated outside of the academy.

Hearn's observation that knowledges are connected to power networks has allowed him to interrogate some of the contemporary discourses around masculinities such as spiritualist discourses. He exposes how neglecting the category of men's power engenders the type of discourses produced by authors such as Bly and some men's rights advocates. In these engagements with men there is a 'political alliance and personal attachment between the author and the men who are addressed in the texts' (Hearn 1998a: 792). In such texts Hearn highlights how the author identifies with the experiences and problems facing modern men as a categorical group, and highlights how these texts reach out to other men who are constructed as facing particular problems. Significantly, the problems associated with men in these texts are constituted by the authors through politically conservative frames.

The absence of theorisations of men's power in these perspectives means that they 'develop anti-feminist perspectives that criticise feminism's effects on men and promote anti-feminist alliances among men' (Hearn 1998b: 793). Therefore, 'men are referred to explicitly but not necessarily problematized, and little, if any, exploration of power relations or the social constitution of the very category of "men" is provided' (792). Bly and men's rights groups, as previous chapters have discussed, often operate with essentialist notions about men which means, as Hearn recognises, they downplay the category of power, and these discourses also support definitions of men's identity as static and predetermined. This standpoint acts to naturalise men's power.

Hearn argues that studies that focus on the limiting effects of the 'male role' may also produce anti-feminist effects. In contrast to Bly's analysis of masculinity, 'men's studies' of the 'male role' have usually adopted a social constructionist theory of gender which deconstructs masculinities as a natural category. Studies of this kind de-naturalise men's identities by disrupting claims that the normative ideals of men's subjectivities are biologically determined. Hearn (1998b: 793) notes how examinations of the production of men's roles have attended to the constraining effects of those roles, while failing to engage with issues of men's gender power and the category of men. Attending to these issues, Hearn argues, demands that men recognise their socially dominant position when they analyse their identities and the effects of those identities on the reproduction of patriarchy.

At a more general level men's studies of men within patriarchal systems, according to Hearn, can cause a range of gendered power effects because this form of analysis in the context of men's social dominance may enable men to further their control over the production of gendered knowledges. The power-effects of these knowledges highlighted by Hearn have already been discussed in Chapter 6. They include the possibility of men's appropriation of feminist funding and teaching within the academy, and the potential sidelining of both feminism and women through the widening of 'men's studies'. To deal with the possible negative effects of knowledges of men and masculinities on feminism and women Hearn, through a series of collaborations, developed a framework for critical studies on men, designed to produce critical analyses of men; while reducing the potential power effects of studies of men on other gendered communities (Hearn *et al.* 1983; Hearn and Morgan 1990).

Against a background of 'legitimate fears that "men's studies" will become yet another variation on a well-established patriarchal theme' (Hearn and Morgan 1990: 5), Hearn worked with other analysts to develop a set of principles for studies of men and masculinities (Hearn *et al* 1983; Hearn and Morgan 1990: 203–5). By doing so these writers exposed a further interrogative dimension of profeminism which extended profeminist analysis onto the terrain of its position within existing power networks.

In order to minimise the possible power effects of men's gender knowledges Hearn and Morgan (1990) argue that profeminist studies need to engage in a set of practices to ensure that men's dominance is not a side-effect of investigations into masculinities. Hearn and Morgan also suggest that for studies of men to be critical, writers needed to adopt a profeminist standpoint and fully recognise the broader relationships of power that benefit men both individually and as a group. They (1990: 204) insist that for 'men's studies' of men to be disruptive of existing gender relationships, 'men's critique of men' needs to be 'developed in the light of feminism', and should be gay-affirmative. Reiterating this point in his study *The Violences of Men*, Hearn (1998a: 43) asserts that: 'Men's research in isolation (from feminism) is likely to reproduce some of the knowledge of anti-feminism.' Reflecting this standpoint, Hearn and Morgan (1990) argue that it is important for profeminists to engage in collaborations with feminists in ways that reduce the possible negative effects of studies of men (see also Hearn 1997). Hearn has worked on a number of explorations of gender relationships with particular feminists (e.g. Hearn and Parkin 1988; 1995; Hanmer, Hearn and Bruce 1992, Harlow, Hearn and Parkin 1995; Harlow and Hearn 1996; Hearn and Jyrkinen 2000; Hearn and Pringle with members of CROME 2002). Hearn therefore positions profeminism within gender studies through the framework of critical studies of men and does not locate it as a separate area of study in competition with women's studies.

Therefore, in contrast to Seidler, Hearn and Morgan (1990) argue for a close relationship between profeminism and feminism. By locating profeminism on the same interrogative ground as feminism and gay politics, Hearn and Morgan clearly differentiated their position not only from forms of 'men's studies' but also, it can be argued, from theorists such as Seidler who fail to fully acknowledge the continuing power relationships between men and women.

Hearn has also argued that men have to recognise their relationships to gendered power structures in their formulations of alliances or appropriations of feminism.

> Men are inevitably located as powerful *within patriarchies,* while men's relationship with feminism is inevitably *problematic.* What this means is that, because of men's structural location within patriarchies as members of the oppressor class, we cannot simply announce our alliance with feminism and feminists, as if that is proof of our good intentions.
>
> (Hearn 1992: 5)

Hearn and Morgan (1990: 203–4) therefore conclude that the necessary steps should be taken by men working on men's gender identities to ensure that feminist teaching, research and funding opportunities are respected and actively protected.

Hearn and Morgan make another important point in relation to the place of power in 'men's studies' of men and masculinities that again highlights these writers' alternative standpoint to Seidler. 'Critical, theoretical discussion of men and masculinities must address itself to the forces making for a relative lack of change as well as forces making for change' (Hearn and Morgan 1990: 16). Seidler suggests that the changes around men's identities mean that the focus of profeminism should be on dealing with the 'wounds' created by these changes. Hearn and Morgan claim that the reproduction of men's power within changing social systems must be incorporated into profeminist analysis, if that analysis is to avoid becoming only a partial examination of men's gendered identities. They stress the need for profeminism to examine the continued advantages men accrue in social systems.

For Hearn, charting men's power is fundamental to an understanding of how changes occurring around masculinities have brought new challenges for men. He argues that gendered social conditions may have changed in ways that challenge men's traditional identities and support improvements in women's position; however, he also maintains that men's power persists in contemporary societies. He (1999: 7) writes that 'while there are clearly all manner of changes in process, there is also a profound state of no change, in the sense that the many arenas of power remain persistently in the control of men'.

Hearn, therefore, develops a different approach to the 'costs' of contemporary masculinity to Seidler's articulation of the notion of men's pain through the concept of 'wounding'. The former argues that masculinities have negative effects on men but these effects cannot be understood if gender identities are not located within broader networks of power. For Hearn (1999) the costs of masculinities arise from inequalities of power not from the effects of feminism. Hearn (1999: 7) comments: 'Men's association with power also creates problems for men themselves.' In contrast to Seidler, Hearn believes that feminism is the means through which these power structures can be deconstructed and the negative impacts of masculinities eradicated.

Like Stoltenberg, Hearn argues that men need to be active in gender politics and he stresses the importance of trying to change men's identities. Profeminism therefore 'involves men in both individual and collective change . . . [it] necessitates concrete actions, notably self-criticism and the attempt to change other men, to encourage others to turn their attention to feminist scholarship' (Hearn and Morgan 1990: 204). Hearn also notes that a critical relation to men,

> does not appear out of 'thin air' or just by an act of individual will-power. It rests on the historical development of pro-feminist, anti-patriarchal practices, activities, research and organizing, and positive relations with feminist theory and practice.
>
> (Hearn 1997: 52)

For Hearn a range of critical, discursive and political practices are available to men that recognise the broader networks that constitute masculinities and within which men's agency occurs. Such practices engender more critical studies on men. He writes that critical studies of men combine,

> a number of elements: a critical relation to the topic, encompassing a self reflexivity of the author, an awareness of both the social location of the author and the topic, and the consideration of the social bases of knowledge; a commitment to the political emancipation of both women and men; and where appropriate, empirical enquiry not just assertion and speculation.
>
> (Hearn 1998b: 801)

Hearn (1998b: 795) includes Stoltenberg's deconstruction and rejection of normative masculinities in the orbit of critical studies of men; although he does note Stoltenberg's categoricalism. Hearn also defines studies that expose the way in which gender connects with other forms of power to produce subjugated forms of masculinities as potentially critically engaged with men's identities (1998b: 797–98). He argues that these kinds of approaches to men's identities engage in the practice of 'alterity.' 'Alterity' involves a move from 'internal uncertainty, to reconstituted positioning, and thus a modified subversion of men' (1998b: 798). Through this strategy men are interrogated as *other.*

For example black, ethnic or gay men's identities are read through their positioning in dominant gendered frameworks. Such interrogations of men's identities have dual effects. They subvert dominant forms of masculinities by exposing how their constitution requires the relational subjugation of other men's identities and they expose the processes through which those identities are subjugated. These studies, Hearn argues, operate as 'a form of resistance to dominant formations of men,' and subvert categorical essentialism (799). Other critical strategies for men include exposing the relationships between men, power and gender through alliances with feminism, as well as subverting and challenging gendered relationships at public and personal levels.

However, even when studies of men reflect the 'baseline' principles of critical studies of men, the effects of knowledges produced by men about their gendered identities have to be constantly assessed. Hearn recognises that at a personal level individuals need to examine and re-examine their relationships to men's radical gender politics. Rather than viewing this process as debilitating, Hearn articulates it as an ongoing and integral practice within studies on men thereby cogently making the case for a reflective approach to knowledge production within profeminism.

Hearn has been keen to develop this approach in his own studies of men and masculinities. For example in his (1998a) study of men's violence to known women, Hearn recognises the possible political effects of such a study in social contexts where men have traditionally been given 'centre stage' in academic analysis. He (1998a: 59) writes that in this type of profeminist study the potential danger is that men 'are being reaffirmed as people (men) of interest to other men, as at the centre of things. Critical Studies of Men need to recognise such temporary re-centrings of/in discourses, and attend to their decentring'.

Consequently, Hearn (1998b: 806), has recognised that men's theorising about men 'needs to be understood as provisional'. Overall he suggests that profeminism does not only have to ensure that its critique of men is critical in the context of broader power structures but he also highlights the need for fluid political and research agendas, which are flexible enough to shift in order to respond to concerns about men's epistemological practices as they emerge.

Hearn's analysis of 'men's studies' of men casts doubt on Stoltenberg's suggestion that resistance to masculinity can be forged through the rejection of men's power. Hearn illustrates how men's resistances to normative gendered identities and gender power are produced through identities that are constituted within networks of power. Men's identities therefore engender particular subversive strategies within particular contexts that impact on the political structuring and effects of profeminism. For Hearn there is no position that profeminism can adopt that is prior to power or beyond power. Rather he suggests that resistance to normative gender identities and gender power is developed through networks of power and this means that such politics always involves risks and unintended power-effects.

Overall, Hearn develops a more complex understanding of the political aspects of forging political resistances within the arena of gender power. This complexity not only emerges from his reflections on critical knowledges and activism by profeminists, but also emerges from the insight that politics does not arise from something intrinsic to masculinity, an authentic or damaged self. It becomes engendered through the political constitution of the category of men within inequitable power structures which produces that category as a political site for oppositional politics.

As a result of this insight the profeminist dimension of the new politics of masculinities cannot be viewed as only subversive of power because the basis of profeminist political resistance, men, is a product of power, always political and implicated in the reproduction of the power structures and the normative subjectivities it resists. Hearn's standpoints on power, men and resistance has also influenced his approach to analysing the terrains of profeminist politics and profeminist practices of resistance at public and private levels. The next section considers these aspects of his theoretical and political frameworks.

Public/private arenas and the politics of changing men

The framework of critical studies on men provides the epistemological orientation for Hearn's analysis of men's individual and collective relation to private and public networks of power. Throughout his studies Hearn interrelates personal subjectivity and everyday life with broader systems of systematic power relationships between men and women. By doing so he exposes the connections between action at the micro-level and macro-level structures. Hearn's analysis of public and private arenas of gender power, in turn, shapes his assessment of arenas and practices of transformation for profeminism.

In his study of transformations in the public sphere, Hearn (1992) shifts his analysis towards an investigation of men's ongoing social dominance in public sphere institutions. The personal aspects of men's identities are to some extent displaced in this study to allow for a more fully focused analysis of the public aspects of gender power. 'This study is inevitably dealing with less than half the story: it isn't possible to do everything all the time' (Hearn 1992: 7). However Hearn's analysis of the public sphere is still linked to changes in men's everyday lives and identities. He (1992: 1) describes his analysis of the public sphere as 'intensely personal' and 'political' emanating from a concern to 'understand and change myself and other men, our social locations, and politics'.

In this study Hearn attempts to provide a more thorough analysis of systematic macro-level gendered structures of power, and considers men's relationship to these structures. He examines changes in the public sphere between 1870 and 1920, a period of economic and social transformations, to expose how these changes allowed men to secure more dominance through public sphere structures – a dominance that he suggests continues in the contemporary societies. Hearn illustrates how, despite social change, men remain in control of public institutions and he charts the way that a public sphere, dominated by men, has increasingly extended its control over private arenas.

Hearn shows how the extension of state intervention in the family, child welfare, sexuality, the growth of organisations, the mass media, the development of informatics, processes of professionalisation, and cultural changes in the period under study both increased men's public power and extended public power over private arenas. Through this kind of analysis he exposes the asymmetries of power between men and women at the public level which counters claims that the 'crisis of masculinity' represents a transition of power from men to women. Challenging that thesis Hearn provides a convincing analysis of the public sphere that suggests that social changes have actually increased men's power within and over social institutions.

He (1992: 3) also notes that men's 'individual power accrues from the general, that is a social structural, relation of men to women, in the public domains and elsewhere'. However he illuminates how men's power at the private level has been undermined by the activities of public groups of men. He (1992: 229) therefore recognises differences in men's relationship to modes of public power, arguing that: 'Men are increasingly a universal world gender class and increasingly fragmented, beyond even identity.'

His analysis of men's dominance in the public sphere exposes the public arena as an important site for transformative politics. He (1992: 231) writes: 'We can certainly challenge and organise against dominant modes of public men—attempt to challenge and change them—by pro-feminist politics against violence, torture, brutality, war, heterosexism.' This concentration on the interrelations between the public/private spheres of gender power also means that he identifies areas where resistance may emerge within patriarchal systems.

As already mentioned, Hearn contends that one notable effect of changes in the public sphere has been that more and more private issues are becoming part of public agendas. The continued integration of the private into the public, for Hearn, means that private arenas can become increasingly politicised and subject to incorporation. He (1992: 20) claims the increased 'appearance and significations in the public domains' of private and 'semi-public' gendered relationships, practices and arrangements 'signals possibilities for undermining patriarchy as hidden forms of oppression become visible in public arenas'.

In a range of other studies Hearn directly develops an analysis of the interrelations between men's agency, experiences and broader ideologies and structures of gender power across the arenas of organisations, social care, colonialism, violence and reproductive labour (see e.g. Hearn 1983; 1987; 1998a; 1999; 2005). In these studies he explores more directly the connections between public and private power and the possibilities for gender resistance by men at these levels. Hearn's focus on the personal level of men's power and identities in these studies means that he assesses the role of experience in constituting gender and explores the category of experience in terms of its subversive potential in formulations of profeminism.

For example in *Birth and Afterbirth* (1983) Hearn investigates the power relationships that emerge between men and women in the arenas of reproduction and reproductive labour. Hearn argues that the labour involved in caring for children is unfairly distributed between men and women in the family. This study frames the arena of fatherhood as political, at both the individual and at the macro-levels of social policy, the state and the dominant social discourses surrounding heterosexism, fatherhood and motherhood.

Hearn argues that macro-level institutions support inequalities between men and women in terms of reproductive labour. While this analysis of fatherhood ensures that Hearn recognises the importance of broader structures for understanding the politics of fatherhood, he also highlights the operation of power in this arena at the personal level of material practices. Hearn exposes how men reproduce inequalities through their everyday behaviour by avoiding childcare; or at least by avoiding the less attractive material aspects of caring for children. This study suggests that explorations of fatherhood by men should not simply consider the effect of normative forms of fatherhood on the emotional capacities of men, because fatherhood is an arena of power wherein men reproduce through their agency within broader structures of patriarchy. Hearn illustrates how the norms of fatherhood are underpinned by an unequal gendered division of physical labour in reproductive arenas that are supported by societal arrangements. He therefore frames profeminist work on men's individual identities as fathers as a process under conditions of external controls and organisation.

Contra Seidler, Hearn exposes the importance of moving beyond seeing fatherhood as a way of reconnecting men to their emotions. He illustrates why it is important to trace the power relationships between men and women in reproductive arenas when examining fatherhood and its effects. Hearn argues that even when fatherhood is reconstituted in profeminist directions it remains a site marked by personal and public power relationships. Hearn therefore argues for political engagement by men that challenges the public and private forms of power that create gendered inequalities and support men's control of the reproductive aspects of life.

For Hearn then, men's politics must be both personal and public. At the public level Hearn identifies the state, social policies and other large scale institutions as targets for profeminist resistances to gender power. This is again reflected in his more recent work on fatherhood that examines the relationship between men, fathers and the state (Hearn 2002). At the private level, he outlines a number of critical strategies for men. These strategies include engagement with feminism, the restructuring of relationships between men, women and children, challenging institutional practices, and the adoption of an anti-sexist critical orientation towards men's personal behaviour and ethics. Hearn (1999) argues that the processes of profeminist change are often difficult for men as they involve men in decisions about where they should target activism and about how they should balance personal needs with political commitments. Hearn (1999) argues that these difficulties and ambiguities should not be marginalised or disabling but should be part of the reflective process of profeminist resistances.

In *Birth and Afterbirth* and similar critical studies of men, Hearn implements the category of men's experiences to develop strategies of interrogation in relation to men's identities and social power. For example he has often employed the category of experience in ways that subvert men's personal identities, open possibilities for personal reinvention by men and connect personal experience with macro-level forms of power. Also in his work on emotions in organisations, Hearn (1993) exposes how emotions are constituted within organisational environments, through social rules, specific contexts and historical features that 'make' feelings. He (1993) recognises how men's emotions are always mediated by historical and social forces and contexts. By doing this Hearn exposes how subjectivities produced through networks of power can be instantiated in critical engagements with men's identities to disrupt and challenge normative masculinities. He suggests that men's experiences can act as the material through which resistance to normative gendered identities by profeminists can occur.

The last chapter exposed the importance that Seidler attached to investigations of men's experiences and biographies in profeminist analysis and politics. Hearn develops a different understanding of this category of experience and develops different models of its deployment in profeminist critique. Whereas Seidler suggests that examining experience can expose the 'wounded self,' Hearn (see especially 1998a) recognises that experiences are generative of political accounts of individual action, emotions and feelings. For Hearn experiences are interpreted through political frameworks saturated with social discourses. 'The resort to men's subjectivity is no guarantee of truth, accuracy, knowledge whatsoever. It is contextualised in relations of power. Men's subjective accounts have to be examined carefully within these relations' (Hearn 1998a:67). Recording experiences and talking about experiences, he claims, can also reiterate the logic of sexist discourses and provide anti-feminist explanatory frameworks. For example in his study of men's violences to known women, he (1998a: 212) writes: 'Men's talk about violence is not merely descriptive; it creates social reality for men and women.'

In other words men's experiences are always political. Hearn therefore draws on feminist analysis to engage critically with the category of experience. This strategy contrasts with Seidler's tendency to insulate men's experiences from feminism, which results in a failure to appreciate the interconnections between the category of men's experiences and networks of gender power. Hearn's profeminism breaks with Seidler's partly because he deploys men's experiences within a political rather than a therapeutic framework, although the deployment of experience in Hearn's studies may have therapeutic effects.

Even Hearn's earlier and more structuralist analyses of personal arenas of gender recognised that experience is not simply given but requires interrogation through oppositional gender frameworks. In *Birth and Afterbirth* Hearn (1983: 5) generates an analysis of reproductive work through 'the experience of being at a birth and then writing down some reflections on it'. He (1983: 5) writes that his reflections of his 'experience or non-experience of birth' was a prelude to an attempt to 'clarify' thinking on politics and theory. In this text Hearn ties his own experiences to the broader structures of reproduction, social policies and institutions such as medicine, and he also engages in a reflection on his agency as a father through a feminist standpoint.

Later in his work he (2005) implements the category, personal experience, to explore colonialism. Through an examination of colonialism in Ireland and Finland, Hearn connects his own experiences in these contexts to reflectively explore and expose how the discourses of colonialism operate through interlinking gendered and ethnic modalities of power. Through this analysis Hearn interrogates the effects of colonialism on two levels. He examines the macro-level effects of colonialism on particular societies and how it has been challenged and subverted. He also engages in a personal analysis involving memory work to discuss the effects of colonialism and uses this reflection to explore the differences in men's positioning within colonial and post-colonial contexts. Hearn's has attempted to develop other cross-cultural analyses of gender and more specifically masculinity, exposing the importance of geographical and social space in explorations of gender and men and masculinities (see e.g. Hearn 2006).

Again, Hearn exposes how men's personal experiences can be connected to macro-level analysis and can become the material for subverting the effects of gender, class, ethnic and racial modalities of power. Experience becomes interspersed with macro-level structural analysis. Hearn uses this strategy to expose how the personal is always political, interconnected to broader networks of power.

Power, knowledge and politics

Given the complexities of Hearn's analysis of men, gender and power, it is not surprising that a range of theoretical issues emerge in his work, particularly in relation to his retention of the categories of patriarchy and gender class. Hearn (1992) shifts from more problematic understandings of patriarchy by theorising it as a particular, rather than a universal phenomenon. He therefore theorises systematic forms of gender power as contingent rather than as pre-determined, universal or static. Importantly, Hearn suggests that men's power is not inherent in social systems or an effect of men's intrinsic identities but is historical, shifting, and dependent on specific social, cultural and geographical environments.

Hearn (1992) also pluralises patriarchies by exposing the particular dynamics of different social institutions. Hearn therefore theorises the reproduction of patriarchy as a fragmented and diverse process, with power being reproduced through multiple mechanisms at particular social sites. This reading of patriarchy does not posit power as centralised or coherent but plural and shifting.

As already mentioned the concept of gender class is also fluid in Hearn's analysis of gender power. Although he retains the notion of gender class to encapsulate the effects of patriarchy on identities, he also understands identities within patriarchal systems as diverse and multi-faceted. By doing so he offers a more dynamic reading of the reproduction of patriarchy compared with some other accounts (see Lloyd 1993 for a critical discussion of the concept). More specifically, he overcomes the weaknesses of some conceptualisations of patriarchy and gender class that created homogenised accounts of men and treated patriarchy as a universal system of gender power.

However Hearn's analysis of gender and power through the constructs of patriarchy and gender class raise some analytical questions. In light of the intricacies of tracing gender, power and identity that Hearn's analysis exposes, it seems reasonable to ask if the concepts of gender class and patriarchy can conceptually support the complexity of blended identities and the intersection of multiple modalities of power with gender power. As Hearn himself notes, the existence of multiple identities across the category of men seems to undermine the conceptual integrity of Hearn's categories of patriarchy and gender class. The purpose of retaining the concept seems primarily related to his worry that without it men's shared gender power and advantage may be sidelined.

However, the deployment of the terms patriarchy and gender class in Hearn's work could potentially act to prioritise gender inequities over other forms of oppression, although it is clear that Hearn does not intend this effect. Indeed he actively encourages attention to modalities of power that intersect with gender. However the application of the terms patriarchy and gender class means that other forms of power and identities tend to be positioned as subsidiary to gender identities and gender power. Gender inequities therefore become marked as the most fundamental form of oppression across social groups (see Butler 1990 for a critical discussion).

In response to this problem, post-structuralist perspectives on gender have suggested that the term patriarchy is fundamentally flawed (see Lloyd 1993). Post-structuralist theorists have suggested that analysts should focus on the intersection of modalities of power in particular contexts rather than implement concepts that suggest that power has a singular logic or direction (see Laclau and Mouffe 1985; Butler 1990; Lloyd 1993; 2005). Certainly Hearn's analysis appreciates different modalities of power and therefore does not view power as having a single logic. However, such perspectives may provide interesting frameworks and insights that could be developed by profeminists to further refine the analysis of the relationships between identity, gender and power.

While certain aspects of Hearn's approach to men, gender and politics may raise some possibilities for further political and theoretical reflections, overall Hearn succeeds in framing profeminism as a political movement forged through political networks, and involved in generating political effects. He theorises the category of men, the 'we' of profeminist politics as an effect of political analysis not as a pre-given biological or experiential category. Hearn's work suggests that the category of men, which is the focus of profeminist politics is not prior to politics but rather emerges from an ethical analysis of the systematic and general gender mechanisms of power. The constitution of the category of men in Hearn's work is therefore a generative, political move to identify arenas for political intervention and to develop strategies of gender transgression across arenas of gender power by men.

The 'we' of profeminist activism is framed in Hearn's work as a political response to the constitution of men's gender identities and men's dominant social positioning. For Hearn profeminism is an ongoing ethical standpoint underpinned by practices designed to increase gender justice. He suggests that profeminism cannot precede politics; it is not grounded in extra-political authentic selves or shared authentic experiences, rather it is an effect of the interrelationships between power and resistance. For Hearn profeminist interventions demand a critical, reflective politics and provisional normative foundations. He highlights the need for profeminism to be flexible enough in its theory and practice to shift in relation to the unintended effects of men's radical gendered politics.

For Hearn men cannot escape gender power in contemporary contexts but must forge a politics of transgression by developing forms of gender resistance from within culturally constituted subjectivities. Illustrating how these subjectivities can reproduce gender power has been a substantial part of his analysis of men, but he also highlights how aspects of subjectivity can be deployed as the material for change and reinvention. Hearn therefore offers a model of profeminism that is closely tied to feminism, is both public and private, and moves profeminist activism beyond models that posit a male positive approach or revolve around rejections of men's identities and power.

The next chapter outlines the work of another writer on men, gender, power and profeminism, Raewyn Connell, who has also attempted to rethink profeminism beyond these models. It illustrates Connell's affinities with aspects of Hearn's analysis of gender and power. Indeed, as will shortly become evident, some of the criticisms that have been directed at Connell's analysis of gender apply equally to Hearn's work. However, the following chapter also examines the distinctive elements of Connell's approach to theorising men, power and profeminist politics, by paying particular attention to Connell's concept of hegemonic masculinity (Hearn 2004).

10 Raewyn Connell

Masculinities, power and alliance politics

> What we are moving towards is indeed 'something rich, & strange'; and therefore, necessarily, a source of fear as well as desire.
>
> R.W. Connell (1995: 234)

Connell, like Hearn, is one of the leading authorities on men and masculinities research. Connell has never identified as a profeminist, and has positioned herself as a socialist before and after her public identification as a transgendered person. However in a number of influential texts, Connell developed and devised a broad theoretical framework for analysing masculinities that has had wide, interdisciplinary, theoretical appeal (1987; 1995; 2000). More specifically, this framework has been highly influential in profeminist studies of men and masculinities. Connell has also developed a particular model of profeminist activism at the personal and public level of politics.

The influence of Connell's *Masculinities* (1995), is testimony to her impact on thinking about men as a gendered category. In this work Connell developed an approach to studying masculinity that appropriated Gramsci's (1971) concept of hegemonic. Connell reworked Gramsci's class analysis of hegemony to theorise relationships both between men and women and between men. Gramsci argued that the ruling class legitimise their dominance primarily through ideological persuasion rather than physical force. Achieving ideological hegemony, Gramsci argued, involves gaining ideological dominance through struggles with competing, counter-hegemonic groups. Gramsci, therefore, highlighted the centrality of ideological struggles and alliances in the process of building hegemony. By doing so he framed the arena of ideology as an important site in oppositional political struggles. Moreover he argued for a strategy of building counter-hegemonic blocs that challenge the legitimacy of the dominant ideologies of capitalism. Connell (especially 1987; 1995; 2000) employed elements of Gramsci's theory to develop a theory of masculinities. More specifically, Connell tries to identify the hegemonic ideals of masculinity and assesses the possibilities of constructing counter-hegemonic strategies of resistance to the dominant ideology of manhood.

Drawing on Gramsci, one of Connell's primary concerns has been to explore how relationships of dominance and subordination are accepted between men and women and among men. Connell embedded this exploration in a theory of gendered power relations that charts inequities between men and women and between different masculinities within their historical contexts. One of Connell's central theoretical claims is that certain ideals of masculinity become hegemonic and a range of other masculinities interact with this dominant model. Connell (Connell and Messerschmidt 2005) has revised the concept of hegemonic masculinity to take account of some weaknesses in the original formulation of the concept. She (see 2005) has also expanded her work to encompass new emerging issues in masculinities research. This chapter concentrates on Connell's analysis of masculinities, her theorisation of private and public forms of power and the transformative forms of politics that emerge from Connell's theorisations of gender, power and hegemonic masculinity.

As Chapter 8 noted, Connell has been critical of perspectives on masculinities that reduce the analyses of these identities to psychological processes thereby engendering therapeutic solutions to gender inequalities. Connell's tracing of the connections between masculinities and power draws her closer to the analytical and political perspectives of Hearn and Stoltenberg. However Connell highlights areas of disagreement with Stoltenberg, and there are some conceptual differences in terms of Hearn and Connell's analysis of masculinities. These differences and disagreements will be fleshed out later in the chapter. The chapter begins, however, by examining Connell's theorisation of men's identities. It then moves on to Connell's analysis of macro and micro-levels of gender power and concludes by assessing the kind of political practices that Connell recommends for men engaged in oppositional gender politics.

Multiple masculinities and power

Connell's theory of hegemonic and multiple masculinities had its origins in reports from an empirical study of inequality in Australian high schools, and related discussions that analysed the making of masculinities and men's bodies (Connell and Messerschmidt 2005). An outline of the concept appeared in an article 'Towards a New Sociology of Masculinity' that criticised sex role theory, and proposed an alternative model of multiple masculinities, located within a broader framework of gendered power relationships (Carrigan, Connell and Lee 1985). Subsequently, the model of multiple masculinities was integrated by Connell into a systematic sociological theory of gender (Connell and Messerschmidt 2005).

Connell's (1987; 1995; 2000) theory of masculinities is underpinned by an analysis of gender that understands masculinity as inherently social and historical, constituted through the contingent practices of normative gender identities, which are (re)produced and structured through power relationships. For Connell practices of masculinity operate to engender inequalities between men and women but because masculinities are historically constituted, they can be modified and changed. Connell defines masculinities as 'configurations of practice structured by gender relations. They are inherently historical; and their making and remaking is a potential process affecting the balance of interests in society and the direction of change' (1995: 44). More specifically, Connell argues that masculinity simultaneously refers to a 'place' that the subject is positioned in within contexts of power. It also encompasses the practices of subjects within that place and the effects of those practices on 'bodily experience, personality and culture' (Connell 1995:71). By theoretically positioning masculinity as a place within systems of power she expands the analysis of masculinity beyond gender role theory by locating the concept within broader systems of power.

Connell (1995) maintains that because masculinity is a configuration of social practice rather than an inherent identity, theories that produce definitions of masculinity as having an essential core, or producing ontological accounts of men, have to be rejected. Connell argues that masculinity is a relational term that only exists in contrast to what it is not, namely femininity; it is not predetermined or pre-cultural. Subsequently, Connell suggests that semiotic analyses of masculinities are helpful because they expose the way in which cultures are marked by broad discursive gendered binaries; but these theoretical frameworks as developed by post-structuralist and post-Lacanian writers, Connell argues, cannot grapple with the analysis of masculinities in more concrete, everyday and institutional spaces (Connell 1995: 71).

However Connell believes that the insight that identities are relational and connected is important in theorising gender and masculinity. Connell (1995: 71) argues that 'no masculinity arises except in a system of gender relations'. Therefore masculinity, for Connell (1995: 74) is a configuration of practice within socially organised arenas of power between men and women wherein women are subordinated, particularly in arenas of production wherein gender divisions of labour are common, and in the arena cathexis wherein 'sexual desire and emotion are shaped'. However masculinity, for Connell, must be pluralised to take account of relationships between men in social arenas.

Connell argues that Gramsci's concept of hegemony, when applied to gender relationships, helps to develop the analysis of masculinities. It can be employed in gendered analysis to explain how certain ideals of masculinity become 'exalted' and legitimised: in other words it enables theorists to understand both how forms of masculinity become hegemonic and operate to justify unequal relationships between men and women more broadly.

> Hegemonic masculinity can be defined as the configuration of gender practice which embodies the currently accepted answer to the problem of the legitimacy of patriarchy, which guarantees (or is taken to guarantee) the dominant position of men and the subordination of women.
>
> (Connell 1995: 77)

Hegemonic masculinity, Connell argues, emerges in the practices and values of powerful men, although powerful men may not exhibit hegemonic masculinity in their everyday behaviour. It is also evident in certain 'exemplars' of dominant masculinities such as film stars (Connell 1995: 77). She (1997: 8) writes: 'In our society, hegemonic masculinity is heterosexual, aggressive and competitive, and homosocial (excluding women from its social networks). It emphasizes hierarchy and the capacity to dominate other men.' As such it 'embodies the currently successful strategy for subordinating women' (1997: 8). However, Connell stresses that hegemonic masculinity is historically shifting and is open to change and challenge.

> When the conditions for the defence of patriarchy change, the bases for the dominance of a particular masculinity are eroded. New groups may challenge old solutions and construct a new hegemony. The dominance of *any* group of men may be challenged by women. Hegemony, then, is a historically mobile relation.
>
> (Connell 1995: 77)

Very few men, Connell argues, meet the standards of hegemonic masculinity. Large numbers of men, however, have some connection to this model and benefit from the 'patriarchal dividend' it produces. This concept refers to 'the advantage men in general gain from the overall subordination of women' (Connell 1995: 79).

Given that identities are blended and multifaceted, Connell argues that men have different relationships to the dominant or hegemonic models of masculinity. Connell marks three different relationships by men to the dominant ideals of masculinity. Groups of men, such as gay men, are subordinated in relation to hegemonic masculinity. As heterosexuality is a central aspect of dominant masculinity, men who do not conform to normative heterosexuality 'are expelled from the circle of legitimacy' (Connell 1995: 79). Other groups of men are complicit with the dominant ideal of manhood. These men are not the 'frontline troops' of patriarchy, their relationships with women and their roles as fathers, Connell (1995: 79–80) argues, means that they have to compromise extensively with women. However these men still benefit from dominant ideals about manhood in terms of 'honour, prestige and the right to command. They also gain a material dividend. In the rich capitalist countries, men's average incomes are approximately double women's average incomes' (Connell 1995: 82).

Connell also highlights how the 'gender order' interplays with other structures of power such as race and class. For example 'race relations may become an integral part of the dynamic between masculinities' (Connell 1995: 80). Subsequently certain class or ethnic groups of men become marginalised in relation to the dominant ideals. 'Hegemonic masculinity among whites sustains the institutional oppression and physical terror that have framed the making of masculinities in black communities' (Connell 1995: 80). Connell shows how black masculinities also play a symbolic role in the constitution of white hegemonic masculinities. Connell (1995: 80) argues: 'In a white-supremacist context, black masculinities play symbolic roles for white gender construction. For instance, black sporting stars become exemplars for masculine toughness'.

Therefore, for Connell (1995: 72), men and women's practices do not consist of isolated practices but are 'configured into larger units'. Connell thus locates configurations of gender practices within the broader gender order. She reveals the existence of multiple masculinities and highlights power relationships between these groups. These configurations and relationships, she suggests, are open to resistances through disruption and transformation (84). Broader 'crisis tendencies' within the gender order implicate masculinities, for Connell, and may provoke, for example attempts to 'restore dominant masculinity' (1995: 84). There are also processes of resistance across the terrain of plural masculinities by, for example the gay movement, and of course, masculinities have been challenged by the feminist movement. The existence of crisis tendencies in the gender order and counter-hegemonic forces mean that 'there could be a struggle for hegemony, and older forms of masculinity might be displaced by new ones' (Connell and Messerschmidt 205: 883). Through an analysis of gender power that examines the relationships between masculinities and gender power in private and public arenas, Connell attempts to identify arenas for resistance to hegemonic forms of masculinities and their effects.

Public and private power

Connell argues that gender power is a systematic form of power that is both dynamic and historically (re)produced. While remaining unconvinced that gender relationships and masculinities are in a state of widespread crisis, she argues that patriarchal systems have exhibited crisis tendencies across certain arenas due to economic, ideological and social changes (Connell: 1995: 84). She (1995: 85) maintains that power relationships show the 'most visible evidence of crisis tendencies'. Connell (1995: 85) contends that the global movement for the emancipation of women combined with 'a historical collapse of the legitimacy of patriarchal power' in ways that established the gender order in rich industrialised countries. Both processes were fuelled by the contradictions that arose from the reproduction of inequitable relationships between men and women and the 'universalising logics of modern state structures and market relations' (1995: 85). Here Connell seems to refer to the logics of neo-liberal economies and the rights-based discourses of liberal democracies that generate models of universal formal equalities of citizenship.

Connell argues that struggles emerged around the legitimation of gender inequalities in these political and economic contexts. Men's different responses to feminism are one kind of expression of struggle around the legitimacy of gender relationships. Some men engaged in a backlash form of politics through fathers' rights groups. Therefore, according to Connell, we can view masculinities as reconfigured through these crisis tendencies as progressive and regressive forms of gender politics interact. Connell also points to how productive relations have also undergone gendered changes. She highlights how increases in women's employment have engendered changes in men's relationship to the workplace. Connell (1995: 85) views relations of cathexis as another arena of transformation. Lesbian and gay sexualities now operate as alternatives to heterosexuality; and heterosexual practice has been affected by women's demands for 'sexual pleasure and control of their own bodies' (1995: 85). Changes in this arena, Connell (1995: 85) maintains, have created tensions around sexuality and men's traditional sexual rights for example, as husbands.

Despite these crisis tendencies, Connell argues that men's dominance and gender inequalities continue to be widespread (Connell e.g. 1987; 1995; 2000; 2005; Connell and Messerschmidt 2005). Connell argues that to understand and challenge gender power across the terrain of masculinities, multiple sites and levels of power need to be analysed.

For Connell, the relationships between power and masculinities can be analysed across four main social dimensions: at the global level of transnational arenas, such as world politics, transnational business and media; at the regional level of culture or the nation-state; at the local level of face to face interactions in families and organisations; and in the arena of bodily reflex practices (e.g. Connell and Messerschmidt 2005). Moreover she fleshes out strategies of resistance within these arenas.

Connell (2005: 40) writes that the arenas of international trade, international relations and global markets are 'arenas of gender formation and gender politics' and constitute 'a world gender order'. The global level of the gender order, Connell (2000: 41) claims, connects 'the gender regimes of institutions, and the gender orders of local society on a world scale'. Connell (2005) argues for example that global processes such as imperialism, decolonisation, neo-colonialism and world markets remake gendered orders within local contexts. Colonialism, for example, had a massive impact on indigenous gender orders (1998: 2000). The new 'global factory' has also remade gendered divisions of labour in different local contexts. Neo-liberalism, for Connell, dominates the global order and its ideology 'closes down possibilities for gender reform' (2000: 53). The global gender order also reaches down into the more private arenas of life, for example, by distributing men's bodies through migration and positioning them in postcolonial arenas of labour (2005: 82). However global forces do not simply impose gender orders on regional and local cultures, they interact with them, as do subjectivities and bodies.

Connell argues that it is more likely that hegemonic masculinity will dominant at the global level. This concept refers to the dominant form of masculinity that 'embodies, organizes, and legitimates men's domination in the world' (Connell 1995: 82). This model of masculinity is associated with business executives, political executives, and those who control its dominant institutions. Connell (1998; 2000; 2005) calls this particular configuration of masculinity transnational business masculinity and claims that it replaced models of bourgeoisie masculinity that were embedded more in local organisations and local conservative cultures. Transnational businesss masculinity is marked by egocentrism, conditional loyalties and a declining sense of responsibility (Connell 2000: 52).

For Connell (1998; 2005) processes of resistance to global gendered orders are already operative, not only at the level of local cultures but also on a more global scale. Feminism has established a strong presence in international organisations such as the United Nations. Critiques of masculinities have emerged through organisations such as NOMAS and reforms around masculinities have appeared in Scandinavian countries. The global gender order is also marked by instabilities that arise from queer politics and the movement of women into previously all male networks (Connell 2000: 83).

As highlighted above, Connell argues that local and micro-level forms of gender power and a range of plural masculinities are connected to the global gender order. However these levels of power and identity constitution also have their own power dynamics, as Connell (e.g. 1995; 2000) illustrates in her ethnographic studies. At local levels masculinities operate through diverse arenas such as schools, hospitals, businesses and friendship groups. At the regional level masculinities are supported by, for example, the ideologies and activities of the state, by regional gendered discourses and social policies. At these levels masculinities become constituted through the diverse economic, political, social and discursive forces that operate in these contexts. At regional and local levels Connell suggests that masculinities are forged in relation to hegemonic masculinity. In these arenas Connell maintains that there are always points for resisting masculinities and the forces that constitute men's identities at different social sites.

Connell (1995; 1998; 2000; 2005) also argues that men's bodies should be located in a political rather than a biological arena. While she argues that on one level bodies have material aspects, many aspects of bodies are constituted, for example, through sports and forms of disciplinary regimes in schools, and as has been highlighted, through the effects of global forms of power. As the body is constituted through social power Connell identifies it as an arena of resistance. At the level of the body, Connell (2000: 65) writes that 'masculine embodiment is an arena for politics, open to change and constantly affected by social power. It is therefore possible to conceive of a *democratic politics* of masculine embodiment, a politics directed towards social justice and peace.'

Areas for reform include remaking masculine embodiment in schools, reducing alcoholism, and reducing practices of violence. Connell (2000: 66) maintains bodily reform also involves more caring and equalitarian interactions between bodies combined with an exploration of greater diversity of bodily pleasure. At personal and bodily levels, Connell (1995 :220–24; 2000: 205) argues, it is possible for men to refuse hegemonic masculinity through rejections of hegemonic masculinity and through the strategic goal of 'recomposing the elements of gender; making the full range of gender symbolism and practice available to all people'.

On the basis of this analysis Connell, like Hearn, argues that the analysis of men's identities has to be located in private and public networks of gender power that benefit men. She outlines sites of resistance within these arenas and suggests that taking on feminist principles means reconstructing personal relations as well as public life. She adds: 'it is often easier to acknowledge women's rights to equal treatment in the public world than to confront sexism at the personal level' (Connell 1997: 7). Men in various institutions can find it easy to support gender equality if it fits their agendas of, for example, modernisation. 'They are less likely to change the power structures of their own personal relationships' (Connell 1997:7).

Before concluding this section it can be noted that while Connell's analysis of transnational masculinities emerges from a broad sweep of global processes, as indicated above, Connell has supported her theory of masculinities through empirical studies at local and bodily levels. This analysis exposed the formation of different masculinities in different social contexts and traced the processes involved in the production of boys and men (Connell 1995; 2000). Both studies involved examining men's articulation of their experiences which Connell subjected to feminist-influenced analysis. Therefore Connell, like Hearn, exposes how men's experiences can become the material for analyses of men's identities and the relationships between these identities and power.

Alliance politics

As already highlighted, the development of the theory of hegemonic masculinity implies that counter-hegemonic forms of masculinity can be developed through challenging the dominant ideals of masculinity at private and public levels and the gender relationships it provokes. Connell (Connell and Messerschmidt 1990: 883) writes that the theory of hegemonic masculinities, when originally formulated, suggested that 'it was perhaps possible that a more humane, less oppressive, means of being a man might become hegemonic, as part of a process leading toward an abolition of gender hierarchies'.

As indicated above, Connell believes that gender relationships are being resisted at different levels of the gender order and suggests that hegemonic masculinity is being challenged. For Connell men can be involved in this democratisation of gender. She warns that such a strategy should avoid the 'me-too mould that characterises some forms of men's gender politics' (1997: 9). She argues that what is required of men involved in radical gender politics is 'quite simply, a commitment to social justice' (1997: 9).

She maintains that because there are diverse forms of patriarchy at different sites, there are many ways to contest them, for example in the workplace, in formal politics, and in reproductive politics. She (1997: 9) asserts that if 'conventional gender is, as sociologists call it "an accomplishment" – something made by the way we conduct ourselves – then we can certainly accomplish something better'.

Connell sets out an agenda of change for men that involves activities such as sharing equal care for children, working to change the workplace to ensure a gender balance between men and women in decision-making positions, confronting homophobia and gay bashing, acting to make sexism, violence towards women and sexual assault 'discreditable'. She also suggests that men become involved in organising political and economic support for women's shelters and rape crisis centres and supports men in their attempts to change curricula in universities and schools to include women's ideas and experiences (Connell: 1997: 9). These strategies challenge the material and ideological dimensions of gender inequalities but they also involve men in a process of rejecting the ideals of dominant forms of masculinities.

However, Connell argues that men should not engage in building a men's movement. The movement model, she maintains is appropriate for stigmatised identities who want to reclaim that identity in oppositional and positive ways. In contrast, for men hegemonic masculinity is not stigmatised. Moreover, 'seeking the unity of "men" can only mean emphasizing the experiences men have that separate them from women, rather than the interests they share with women that might lead towards gender justice' (Connell 2000: 209). Indeed Connell suggests that pursuing gender justice may involve sharp divisions between men, as the standpoint and campaigns of profeminism, generally, will be interpreted as being against men's interests by other men (2000: 210). Therefore 'anti-sexist politics must be a source of disunity among men, not a source of solidarity' (1995: 236). Furthermore she argues that anti-sexist politics is unlikely to generate support from the majority of men who have an interest in maintaining their gender privilege. Connell also warns that men's groups that have operated around agendas of male solidarity and 'male positivism' have tended to 'abandon issues of social justice' (Connell 1995: 236).

Concerned about the effect of certain men's groups, Connell recommends an alternative model of alliance politics for anti-sexist men. She argues that some people think that masculinity politics requires a 'men's movement' but this is not the case. Alliance politics 'may be found outside of pure gender politics at the intersections with other structures' (Connell 1995: 237). Opportunities for men to engage in politics emerge in struggles where men pursue solidarity with women in a similar situation – for example in unions, community politics, anti-colonial movements and movements for racial equality' (1995: 237). Connell cites a number of progressive alliances by men and women in different countries that expose the progress that can be made in terms of gender politics across the terrain of class and racial politics. Politics across these dual arenas of identity, Connell claims, necessarily involves 'joint action with women,' and will 'bring to light the conflicting interests of different groups of men' (1995: 238).

Connell (1995: 238) argues that an orientation towards 'ideological purity' in the work of Stoltenberg, for example, tends to denounce such strategies as involving containment and compromise. Connell rejects this standpoint arguing that pluralism in gender politics is important, and containment is not its necessary outcome. Furthermore she argues that men are likely to be 'detached from the defence of patriarchy in small numbers at a time, in a great variety of circumstances' (2000: 210). She concludes that rather than 'a grand "men's movement", men should be thinking about the possibilities of a variety of struggles linked through networking rather than mass mobilization or formal organization' (2000: 210).

Here Connell tries to reduce the possibility of profeminist resistance moving towards introspective forms of politics that operate primarily around the positioning of men, and run the risk of eclipsing women and other forms of social grievances. For Connell however men's groups remain important for reasons of support. Connell suggests then, that masculinity politics should become part of an alternative historic bloc that struggles against hegemonic masculinities and multiple forms of inequalities.

Connell exposes opportunities for politics that intersect around multiple modalities of power, exposing gender as thoroughly interconnected with other social inequalities. Yet, alliances with women are no guarantee of moving beyond power relationships; indeed, some feminists' critiques of the White Ribbon Campaign, which Connell frames as an example of alliance politics between women and men, expose the range of issues that surround such interventions. Alliance politics seems to offer an important alternative to forms of politics that operate around the category of men and are inward looking. However, alliance politics in practice does not offer a politics beyond power; it is more likely to be a model that will support progressive political practice but may also engender particular gendered power effects.

What is masculinity?

Connell's strategy of alliance politics has been much less problematic than her theory of hegemonic masculinity. This concept has been the most influential aspect of Connell's analysis of gender but it has also been extensively criticised. This section discusses some of the most significant challenges to Connell's theory of masculinities.

Hearn, for example (1996: 202), argues that the concept of masculinities has 'served as a symbolic icon for the more general increase in interest in the study of men, critical or otherwise.' He (1996; 203) suggests that often the concept is employed in explorations of gender but analysts do not define the meaning of the concept. More pointedly, Hearn (1996: 207) argues that masculinity has become 'some kind of thing in itself.' Similarly Whitehead (2002: 93–94) complains that the individual is 'lost' in the concept of masculinity because it leads to the prioritisation of an 'ideological apparatus' over men's concrete 'identity work'.

Developing this point further, Hearn writes that men's practices become the 'expression' of masculinity. Men's practices are criticised but masculinity is framed as the problem, and men concentrate on reforming their masculinity. 'Instead of wondering whether they should change their behaviour, men "wrestle with the meaning of masculinity"' (Hearn 1996: 207). Most usages of the term masculinity, Hearn maintains, divert attention from men's practices. Particular framings of the term may also suggest that masculinity exists prior to its production through social agency and may reiterate a false dichotomy between masculinities and femininities. Hearn (1996; 2004) argues that the concept of masculinity may not be necessary to the project of analysing men and gender relationships, and proposes that it may be preferable to 'move from "masculinities" back to "men"' (Hearn 1996: 214).

Other theorists have questioned the relationship between masculinity and the exercise of power by men (Holter 1997; 2003; Hall 2002). Holter (1997) argues that hegemonic types of masculinity are not necessarily linked to the personal exercise of power over women. Hall (2002), adopting a different theoretical lens, argues that the marginalised masculinities of working-class men involved in forms of criminal violence cannot be viewed as gaining patriarchal privileges through that violence. He argues for the prioritisation of a class analysis that exposes the material basis of the 'pointless' violence of some working-class men, and blames Connell for suggesting that such violence is an effect of some form of 'archaic lust for power'. Other theorists have complained about the constitution of hegemonic masculinity in purely negative terms (Collier 1998). Collier (1998) suggests that hegemonic masculinity must have some positive aspects.

Other analysts have questioned dimensions of Connell's theory of hegemonic masculinities from a poststructuralist perspective. Wetherell and Edley (1999: 337) wonder about 'the appropriateness of a definition of dominant masculinity which no man can ever embody'. They suggest that hegemonic masculinity has multiple meanings and scholars should focus on how men negotiate, produce and reproduce identities by taking up the multiple meanings of masculinities in particular contexts. They (1999: 352) argue that it is important to trace the discursive strategies men employ to position themselves as part of a constituted category of men and the implications of these self-positionings rather than commencing the analysis of men by defining masculinity as prior to its constitutions (see Jefferson 2002 also).

Petersen (2003) like Hearn (1996) argues that the theory of hegemonic masculinity may reproduce a gender dichotomy between men and women. He (2003: 58) suggests that it is important, through historical deconstruction, to expose the taken-for-granted assumption of a stable gender dualism between men and women by exposing the subject positions that destabilise gendered binaries by 'exposing the extensive variations within each sex'. The problem for Petersen (2003: 60) is that theorists have attempted to denaturalise gender through the 'heterosexist idea that there are only two complementary sexes/genders'.

Connell and Messerschmidt (2005) have responded to these criticisms, and have subsequently revised the framework of hegemonic masculinity to take account of empirical work in the field of masculinity studies and the concerns of other analysts in relation to the original formulation of the concept. They (2005: 851) conclude that it is important that the concept of masculinity is defined in research to reduce the ambiguity of the concept, and that attention is paid to alternative sexualities such a transgendered identities; although they argue that alternative sexualities are not inherently counter-hegemonic. They (2005: 848) also highlight the importance of studying masculinity in relation to women, and acknowledge the need to examine women's resistances (not just compliance) with hegemonic masculinity. Furthermore, (1995: 852) they maintain that 'without treating men as objects of pity, we should recognise that hegemonic masculinity does not necessarily translate into a satisfying experience of life'. Moreover they accept that it may well have positive dimensions. They also highlight their concerns that discursive analysis of masculinity could marginalise the material aspects of men's identities such as economic forces and institutions.

However, Connell and Messerschmidt also reject some criticisms of the original concept. They (2005: 843) refute the claim that the theory of hegemonic masculinity reduces analysis to the level of structural determinism. Connell also notes how Hall's (2002) analysis of working-class criminality sidelines issues of gender by prioritising capitalism as the primary causal factor in working-class criminality. Hall analyses men's violence by heavily marginalising practices such as domestic violence.

Regardless of the criticisms that have been levied at the concept of hegemonic masculinity it is likely that the concept will continue to be employed in analyses of men and power for some time. However, what debates around the concept illustrate is the multitude of issues that are involved in trying to theorise the concepts of men's identities and power. It seems likely that feminism/profeminism will continue to debate these complex concepts and the forms of oppositional politics that emerge around them.

11 Profeminism, Theory and Practice
Reflections

Despite the complexity of the social and political changes that have occurred in the arena of gender relations in late capitalist societies, it is clear that men's traditional identities and dominant social positions have become problematised. Profeminism can be viewed as an effect of that problematisation and as a set of discourses and practices involved in extending that problematisation in complex and politically engaged ways. Against a background of anti-feminist discourses about the victimisation of men and the feminist contamination of, particularly young men, profeminists have developed alternative narratives focused on rethinking men's identities and men's roles within the framework of emancipatory gender politics.

The dual project of reinventing masculinities and challenging structures of gender power means that profeminism offers new and often fresh insights into gender relationships, men's subjectivities and the modes through which gender power is produced. Central to profeminist concerns has been the analysis of identity, power and oppositional politics at private and public levels. Like other forms of identity politics, profeminism attempts to produce oppositional strategies of resistance and knowledge across this conceptual and political terrain. More specifically it explores the fluidity of identity and its relationship to private and public forms of power. Profeminism seeks a politics that engenders changes in traditional formulations of identity and challenges the social anchors of traditional relationships across dominant and subordinate identities. However, as this analysis of profeminism has exposed, the conceptualisation of profeminism's central concepts can lead to different forms of political practice and relationships with feminism.

For example Seidler argues that giving space to the articulation of men's feelings and emotions in a culture that has defined masculinity as detached and unemotional is essential if men are to explore their identities freely and reform them beyond traditional models that oppress women and alienate men from each other. While Seidler deconstructs the traditional model of emotionally detached masculinity as an effect of historical processes, his neglect of power means that he disconnects this exploration from broader gender relations.

Noting the problematic aspects of this formulation of the place of men's experiences and emotions in profeminist discourses and practice does not mean that profeminist politics has to operate across a rationalist discourse that sidelines men's emotional experiences or pain. As other writers discussed in this book have illustrated the concepts of experience and emotion can be discussed within the framework of broader networks of power. For example Hearn's treatment of affective concepts exposes how experience and emotion are effects of power and how their articulation can engender oppositional practices and critical readings of men's 'authentic' views of their biographies and identities.

Identity however is a fluid and complex concept. As this study of profeminism has illustrated, the conceptualisation of men's identity has been an arena of great contention within profeminism. The concept of masculinity has become the main reference point for explorations of men's identities and for formulations of narratives about changing men. While the concept may have been of great analytical use, it requires careful deployment and analytical clarity. If it has become a term that shifts attention from men's actual practices and acts to reify gendered categories, as Hearn suggests, then there may be good reasons for attempting to re-theorise men's identities beyond the term 'masculinities' to produce a more multi-conceptual framework for examining men's subjectivities, bodies and practices.

The concept of power will continue to be fundamental in the development of this framework, as it is in profeminist theory and practice more generally. Several writers discussed in this book expose how individual identity does not revolve around an isolated self. Instead subjectivity is located within broader networks of power, which means that personal reinventions may have implications for others. Moreover acknowledging identities as blended and multifaceted raises issues about the reproduction of heterosexist gendered frameworks of sexual difference in some forms of profeminist discourses and practices.

While a concentration on power differences between men and women may mean that profeminism works within the confines of an illusionary categorical division between men and women, an alternative strategy that exclusively concentrates on exposing the plurality of formulations of gender, sex and desire within and between the categories of men and women creates its own problems. Deconstructive strategies are important but gender politics seems to require an intervention in arenas where there are clear social, economic, legal and political inequities between pluralist communities of men and women. Connell, Hearn and Stoltenberg explore this arena and their analysis is important in terms of charting inequality and thinking through concrete responses to areas where gender relationships produce marked gendered inequalities.

However the association of heterosexual, middle class, white men, in particular, with power and the reproduction of gender inequality does not mean that explorations of men's identities have to be focused only on the negative aspects of those identities or framed through analyses of men as constituting a 'social problem'. Connell notes that the majority of men do not live out the hegemonic model of masculinities, their lives are more complex than hegemonic models can support. Recognising men's diverse loyalties across genders, their practices of care for others and their concepts of familial and communal responsibilities helps expose the diverse range of practices that mark the category of men. Attention to these practices within the category of men does not mean side-stepping issues of power or accountability but it does paint a more complex picture of men's identities in contemporary societies.

This kind of focus does not entail moving towards a 'male positive' standpoint. Such a position suggests that men have some kind of authentic identity that requires positive validation. Similarly an 'anti-male' perspective offers little in terms of conceptual clarity or theoretical usefulness. The one guiding idea in this book has been that men's identities are not intrinsic, rather they are constituted through sets of diverse, changing and often contradictory practices that people socially categorised as men reproduce through their agency within contexts of power. As men's identities do not exist prior to or beyond the social practices and historical forms of subjectivity that generate them, the adoption of 'male positive' or 'anti-male' standpoints makes little sense. It seems more appropriate to evaluate men's agency within networks of power than to celebrate or refuse some concept of authentic shared identity among people identified by society as men.

This exploration of profeminism has also illustrated how discourses and practices revolving around welcoming personal change or engaging in public forms of resistance create a range of problematic effects. Tracing these effects seem central concerns for the profeminist agenda. While no conceptual framework or political strategy can move beyond power relationships, the more disruptive forms of profeminism highlight power and engage with the connections between the public and the personal. More radical forms of profeminism operate at the intersection of these concepts.

Overall this book has attempted to clarify the different formulations of these concepts in profeminism. It has illustrated the way different theories of men, masculinities, power and resistance have led to the development of competing models of politics in profeminism. In terms of the models of politics that profeminism has developed Connell is correct to warn against the adoption of a vision of profeminist politics as a mass movement of men engaged in challenging gender inequities. Such a vision reflects the lure of the ideology of completion. In contemporary social contexts this vision frames profeminism as bound to failure. Given the advantages that men accrue from gender inequities it is unlikely profeminism will entice substantial numbers of men to fight for increases in gender equality. Profeminism's challenges to social inequities and the regulatory ideals of gender as this book has illustrated can be developed through a more modest, provisional, fragmented, and, perhaps most importantly, critically reflective form of politics. Strands of profeminism have much to offer oppositional gender politics. For those men still confused about how to engage with feminist theory and practice, the more radical strands of profeminism offer reflective, critical and engaged models of politics for men who want to be involved in oppositional gender politics.

Notes

2 Men Doing Feminism

1 Notions of sisterhood are usually associated with radical feminism. However, as Lynne Segal (1999: Chapter 1) has outlined, building connections between women was also an important and substantial element in socialist feminism. Socialist and Marxist feminists were much more concerned with analysing the relationships between gender inequality and capitalism than radicals. However the development of dual systems theory supported a theoretical conceptualisation of gender power as a product of the interrelationships between capitalism and patriarchy (see Tong 1989 for further elaboration on these theoretical frameworks).

6 The Problematic of Men and Feminism

1 Radical feminism began to develop a theoretical framework for the purposes of exploring women's oppression in society in the 1960s. The paradigm supports a diverse body of work. Writers working within this school of feminist thought have developed different theoretical frameworks for analysing the constitution of gender, power and resistance and disagreed on how gender relationships should be conceived. The radical feminist writers examined in this chapter have been viewed by some commentators as representing a body of thought that is distinctive from radical feminist theory. Alice Echols claims that radical feminism theorises gender as culturally produced. She claims that some writers who are viewed as representing radical feminist thought, such as Mary Daly, Adrienne Rich, Andrea Dworkin and Catherine MacKinnon are not radical feminists at all. Echols claims that these writers posit essentialist or universalistic theories of gender identity and therefore represent a separate paradigm within feminist thought. Echols calls this paradigm cultural feminism (A. Echols, 1989). While the writers that Echols refers to do construct essentialist notions about gender identity these writers can be viewed as part of the radical feminist paradigm, which can be defined by its desire to develop a theory of gender without reference to any other politics. Radical feminism developed a theory of men's power using conceptual tools developed

by women themselves. Also radical feminists themselves identify these writers as part of their tradition (see D. Bell, and R. Klein, eds., 1996). They will therefore be classified as radical feminists in this discussion. (For further critical commentary on radical feminism see Eisenstein 1984; Grimshaw 1984.)

References

Alpert, J. (1973) 'Mother right: a new feminist theory' *Ms.*, August, 52–55.

Ashe, F. (1999) 'The subject', in F. Ashe et al. *Contemporary Social and Political Theory: An Introduction*, UK: Open University Press, 88–110.

—— (2004) 'Deconstructing the experiential bar: male experience and feminist resistance', *Men and Masculinities*, 7 (2): 187–204.

——(2006a) 'Gendering the Holy Cross School conflict: women and nationalism in Northern Ireland,' *Political Studies,* 54 (1): 147–64.

——(2006b) 'The McCartney sisters search for justice: gender and political protest in Northern Ireland', *Politics,* 26 (3): 161–67.

——(2006c) 'The Virgin Mary complex: feminism and Northern Ireland Politics', *Critical Review of International Social and Political Philosophy,* 9 (4): 573–88.

——(2006d) 'Gender in Northern Ireland', paper presented Gender, Nationalism and Equality Seminar, INCORE, Northern Ireland, March.

Astor, N. (1993) quoted in H. Exley (ed.) *The Best of Women's Quotations*, UK: Exley Giftbooks.

Awkward, M. (1999) *Scenes of Instruction: A Memoir*, Durham, NC: Duke University Press.

Babcock, M. (1995) 'Critiques of co-dependency: history and background issues', in M. Babcock and C. McKay (eds) *Challenging co-dependency: Feminist Critiques*, Toronto: University of Toronto Press.

Banks, S. (1995) 'Fear of fucking'. Online. Available http://www.achilles.-freeuk.com/article22_9.html (accessed 20 March 2006).

Bauroth, N. (2000) 'Real women to our rescue.' Online. Available http://www.mensd.org/liberator/2509/tl25–29-all-htm (accessed 10 March 2000).

Baumli, F. (1985) *Men Freeing Men*, Jersey City, NJ: New Atlantic.

Bly, R. (1990) *Iron John*, Reading, MA: Addison-Wesley.

Braidotti, R. (1987) 'Envy: or with my brains and your looks' in A. Jardine and P. Smith (eds) *Men in feminism*, USA: Routledge, 233–41.

Broad, K.L. (2002) 'Social movement selves' *Sociological Perspectives*, 45 (3), 317–66.

Brannon, D. and David, D. (eds) (1975) *The Forty-Nine Percent Majority*, New York: Addison-Wesley.

Brittan, A. (1989) *Masculinity and Power*, UK: Basil Blackwell.

Brod, H. (ed.) (1987) *The Making of Masculinity: The New Men's Studies*, Winchester, MA: Allen and Unwin.

Buechler, S. (2000) *New Social Movements in Advanced Capitalism: The Political Economy and Cultural Construction of Social Activism*, New York: OUP.

Butler, J. (1990) *Gender Trouble: Feminism and the Subversion of Identity*, USA: Routledge.

Campbell, B. (1993) *Goliath: Britain's Most Dangerous Places*, London: Methuen.

Canaan, J. and Griffin, C. (1990) 'The new men's studies: part of the problem or part of the solution?' in J. Hearn (ed.) *Men, Masculinities and Social Theory*, London: Unwin and Hyman, 206–14.

Carrigan, T., Connell, R. W. and Lee, (1987) 'Toward a new sociology of masculinity', in H. Brod (ed.) *The Making of Masculinity*, Boston, MA: Allen and Unwin, 63–100.

Chapple, S. and Talbot, D. (1990) *Burning Desires*, New York: Simon and Schuster.

Chapman, R. (1988) 'The great pretender: variations on the new man theme', in R. Chapman and J. Rutherford (eds) *Male Order: Unwrapping Men, Unwrapping Masculinity*, UK: Lawrence and Wishart, 225–48.

——and Rutherford (eds) (1988) *Male Order: Unwrapping Men, Unwrapping Masculinity*, UK: Lawrence and Wishart.

Christian, H. (1994) *The Making of Anti-sexist Men*, UK: Routledge.

Clatterbaugh, K. (1990) *Contemporary Perspectives on Masculinity: Men, Women, and Politics in Modern Society*, USA: Westview Press.

Clough, P. (1994) *Feminist Thought*, Oxford: Blackwell.

Collier, R. (1998) *Masculinities, Crime and Criminology: Men, Heterosexuality and the Criminal (ised) Other*, London: Sage.

Collinson, D. L. and Hearn, J. (1996) ' "Men" at "work": multiple masculinities/multiple workplaces', in M. Mac An Ghaill (ed.) *Understanding Masculinities: Social Relations and Cultural Arenas*, UK: Open University Press, 61–76.

——(2005) 'Men and masculinities in work, organisation and management', in M. Kimmel, J. Hearn, R.W. Connell (eds) *Handbook of Studies of Men and Masculinities*, London: Sage, 289–310.

Connell (1987) 'Gender and Power', Sidney: Allen & Unwin.

——(1995) *Masculinities*, UK: Polity Press.

——(1997) 'Men, masculinities and feminism', *Social Alternatives* 16 (3): 7–10.

——(2000) *The Men and the Boys,* Cambridge: Polity.

——(2002) 'On hegemonic masculinity and violence: response to Jefferson and Hall', *Theoretical Criminology*, 6 (1): 89–99.

——(2005) 'Globalization, imperialism and masculinities', in M. S. Kimmel, J. Hearn, J. and R.W. Connell (eds) *Handbook of Men and Masculinities*, London: Sage.

Connell, R.W. and Messerschmidt, J.W. (2005) 'Hegemonic masculinity: rethinking the concept', *Gender and Society*, 19 (6): 829–59.

Craig, S. (ed.) (1992) *Men, Masculinity and the Media*, USA: Sage.

Crook, S., Pakulski, J. and Waters, M. (1992) *Postmodernization: Change in Advanced Society*, London: Sage.

Carrigan, T., Connell, R.W. and Lee, J. (1985) 'Towards a new sociology of masculinity'. *Theory and Society*, 4 (2): 143–59.

Daly, M. (1979) *Gyn/ecology: The Meta-ethics of Radical Feminism*. London: The Women's Press.

——(1984) *Pure lust: Elementary feminist philosophy*. Boston, MA: Beacon.

Della Porta, D. and Dani, M. (1998) *Social Movements: An Introduction*, Oxford: Blackwell.

Digby, T. (ed.) (1998a) *Men Doing Feminism*, USA: Routledge.

Digby, T. (1998b) 'Introduction' in T. Digby (ed.) *Men Doing Feminism*, USA: Routledge, 1–16.

Doyle, R. (1976) *Rape of the Male*, Minnesota: Poor Richard's Press.

——1999. Online. Available http.//www.mensdefenceorg/letter.htlm (accessed 4 May 1999).

Dworkin, A. (1974) *Woman Hating*, New York: Plume.

——(1982) *Our Blood: Prophecies and Discourses on Sexual Politics*, London: The Women's Press.

——(1981) *Pornography: Men Possessing Women*, New York, London: The Women's Press.

——(1986) *Ice and Fire*, London: Fontana.

——(1987) *Intercourse*, New York: Free Press and Macmillan.

——(1990) 'Dworkin on Dworkin', *Trouble and Strife*, 19, 2–13.

Duffell, N. (1997) 'Dancing in the dark'. Online. Available http://www.achillesheel.freeuk.com/article22_8.html (accessed 10 March 2006).

Echols, A., (1989) 'The taming of the id: feminist sexual politics', in C. Vance (ed.) (1989) *Pleasure and Danger: Exploring Female Sexuality*, UK: Pandora Press, 50–72.

Ehrenreich, B. (1983) *The Hearts of Men*, New York: Doubleday.

Eisenstein, H. (1984) *Contemporary Feminist Thought*, London: Unwin.

Emerson, R.W. (1992) 'Woman', in M. Kimmel and T. Mosmiller (eds) *Against the Tide: Pro-feminist Men in the United States 1776–1990*, Boston, MA: Beacon, 217–19.

European Profeminist Men's Network. Online: Available http://www.europrofem.org/02.info/27sites/01.links.htm (accessed 10/April/2005).

Faludi (1999) *Stiffed: The Betrayal of the Modern Man*, UK: Chatto and Windus.

Farrell, W. (1974) *The Liberated Man*, New York: Random House.

——(1993) *The Myth of Male Power*, New York: Simon and Schuster.

Fasteau, M. (1974) *The Male Machine*, New York: McGraw-Hill.

Flood, M. (2002) *The Men's Bibliography*. Online: Available http://mensbiblio.xyonline.net/ (accessed June 2004).

Folbre, N. (1994) *Who Pays For the Kids? Gender and the Structures of Constraint*, London: Routledge.

Foucault (1979a) *Discipline and Punish: The Birth of the Prison*, Harmondsworth: Penguin.

——(1980a) *The History of Sexuality: An Introduction*, Harmondsworth: Penguin.

——(1980b) *Power/Knowledge, 1972–1977*, (ed.) C. Gordon, Brighton: Harvester.

——(1982) 'The subject and power' in H. Dreyfus and P. Rabinow *Michel Foucault: Beyond Structuralism and Hermeneutics*, Hemel Hempstead: Harvester Wheatsheaf, 208–26.

——(1984a) 'Truth and power', in H. Dreyfus and P. Rabinow (eds) *The Foucault Reader*, London: Penguin, 51–75.

——(1984b) 'Nietzsche, genealogy, history', in H. Dreyfus and P. Rabinow (eds) *The Foucault Reader*, London: Penguin, 76–100.

——(1984d) 'What is enlightenment?', in H. Dreyfus and P. Rabinow (eds) *The Foucault Reader*, London: Penguin, 32–50.

——(1984e) 'Polemics, politics, and problemizations: an interview with Michel Foucault', in H. Dreyfus and P. Rabinow (eds) *The Foucault Reader*, London: Penguin, 381–90.

——(1985) *The Uses of Pleasure: The History of Sexuality, Volume 2*, London: Penguin.

—(1986) *The Care of the Self: The History of Sexuality, Volume 3*, London: Penguin.

Fraser, N. (1989a) 'Foucault on power: empirical insights and normative confusions', in N. Fraser, *Unruly Practices: Power, Discourse and Gender in Contemporary Social Theory*, UK: Polity Press.

——(1989b) 'Michel Foucault: a "young conservative"?', in N. Fraser *Unruly Practices: Power, Discourse and Gender in Contemporary Social Theory*, UK: Polity Press, 35–54.

——(1989c) 'Foucault's body language: a posthumanist political rhetoric', in N. Fraser *Unruly Practices: Power, Discourse and Gender in Contemporary Social Theory*, UK: Polity Press, 55–66.

Fuss, D. (1990) *Essentially Speaking: Feminism, Nature and Difference*, London and New York: Routledge.

Gamson, J. (1995) 'Must identity movements self-destruct? a queer dilemma', *Social Problems*, 42 (1): 390–407.

Giddens, A. (1990) *The Consequences of Modernity*, Cambridge and Stanford, CA: Polity Press and Stanford University Press.

—— (1991) *Modernity and Self-Identity: Self and Society in the Late Modern Age*, Cambridge: Polity Press.

—— (1992) *The Transformation of Intimacy: Sexuality, Love and Eroticism in Modern Societies*, Cambridge: Polity Press.

—— (1999) *Runaway World: How Globalisation is Shaping Our Lives*, London: Profile.

Gilder, G. (1973) *Sexual Suicide*, New York: Bantam.
——(1986) 'The princess problem', *National Review*, 28–32.
Goldberg, S. (1974) *The Inevitability of Patriarchy*, New York: William Morrow.
Goldrick-Jones (2002) *Men Who Believe in Feminism*, Westport, CT: Praeger.
Grant, J. (1993) *Fundamental Feminism: Contesting the Core Concepts in Contemporary Feminist Theory*, New York: Routledge.
Grimshaw, J. (1986) *Philosophy of Feminist Thinking*, Minneapolis, MN: University of Minnesota Press.
Gross, N. (2005) 'The detraditionalization of intimacy considered', *Sociological Theory*, 23 (3): 286–311.
Gutterman, D. (1994) 'Postmodernism and the interrogation of masculinity', in H. Brod and M. Kaufman (eds) USA: Sage Publications Inc., 219–38.
Habermas, J. (1981) 'New social movements', *Telos* 49 (Fall): 33–37.
——. (1989) *The Structural Transformation of the Public Sphere*, Cambridge, MA: MIT Press.
Hall, C. S. and Norby V. (1973) *A Primer of Jungian Psychology*, New York: Taplinger.
Hall, S. (2002) 'Daubing the drudges of fury: men, violence and the piety of the "hegemonic masculinity" thesis', *Theoretical Criminology*, 6 (1): 35–61.
Hall, S. and Jacques, M. (eds) (1989) *New Times: The Changing Face of Politics in the 1990s*, London: Lawrence and Wishart in association with *Marxism Today*.
Hagan, K.L. (ed.) (1992) *Women Respond to the Men's Movement*, San Francisco, CA: Harper Collins.
Haraway, D. (1991) *Simians, Cyborgs and Women*, London: Free Association Books.
Hayward, F., (1987) 'A shortage of good women', *Single Scene Magazine*, 12/09/1987.
Heath, M. (2003) 'Soft-boiled masculinity: renegotiating gender and racial ideologies in the Promise Keepers' movement', *Gender and Society* 17 (3): 423–44.
Heartfield, J. (2002) 'There is no masculinity crisis.' Online. Available http://www.genders.org/g35_heartfield.txt (accessed 4 December 2002).
Hearn, J. (1983) *Birth and Afterbirth: A Materialist Account*, London: Achilles Heel.
——Creighton, C., Middleton, C. Morgan, D., Thomas, R. Pearson, C. (1983) 'Changing men's sexist practice in sociology', *Network* 25.
——(1987a) *The Gender of Oppression*, UK: Wheatsheaf.
——(1987b) 'Changing men's studies', *Achilles Heel* magazine, 8 (April) Online. Available http://www.achillesheel.freeuk.com/article10_1.html (accessed 12 November 2002).
Hearn, J. and Parkin, W. (1987 2nd edition 1995) *Sex at Work: The Power and Paradox of Organisational Sexuality*, Brighton: Wheatsheaf; New York: St Martin's Press.

——and Morgan (1990) 'The critique of men', in J. Hearn and D. Morgan (eds) *Men, Masculinity and Social Theory*, Hyman Unwin: London, 203–5.

——(1992) *Men in the Public Eye*, New York & London: Routledge.

——(1993) 'Emotive subjects: organisational men, organisational masculinities and the (de)construction of "emotions" ', in S. Fineman (ed.) *Emotions in Organisations*, London: Sage, 142–66.

Hearn, J. and Collinson, D. (1994) 'Theorising unities and differences between men and between masculinities', in H. Brod and M. Kaufman (eds) *Theorising Masculinities*, Thousand Oaks, CA: Sage, 96–118.

——(1996) 'Is masculinity dead? a critique of the concept of masculinity/ masculinities', in M. Mac An Ghaill (ed.) *Understanding Masculinities; Social Relations and Cultural Arenas*, Buckingham and Philidelpia, PA: Open University Press, 202–17.

——(1997) 'The implications of critical studies on men', *Nora*, 3 (1): 48–60.

——(1998a) *The Violences of Men*, London: Sage.

——(1998b) 'Theorizing men and men's theorizing: varieties of discursive practices in men theorizing of men', *Theory and Society*, 27: 781–816.

——(1998c) 'The welfare of men?' in J. Popay, J. Hearn and J. Edwards (eds) *Men, Gender Divisions and Welfare*, London: Routledge.

——(1999) 'It's time for men to change', in J. Wild (ed.) *Working with Men for Change*, London: UCL Press, 5–15.

——(1999) 'A crisis in masculinity, or new agendas for men', in S. Walby *New Agendas for Women*, London: Macmillan

——(2002) Men, fathers and the state: national and global relations' in B. Hobson (ed.) *Making Men into Fathers: Men and Masculinities and the Social Politics of Fatherhood*, Cambridge: Cambridge University Press, 245–72.

——(2004) 'From hegemonic masculinity to the hegemony of men', *Feminist Theory*, 5 (1) 49–72.

——(2005) Autobiography, nation, post-colonialism and gender relations: reflecting on men in England, Finland and Ireland, *Irish Journal of Sociology*, 14 (2): 66–93.

——and Holmgren L. E. (2006) 'Locating men's diverse gender–conscious positionings on gender, equality and feminism: theoretical frameworks and practical passings', *Feministische Studien* 2: 1–14.

Hearn, J. and Hertta, N. (2006) 'Is there a "men's movement" in Finland? The state of men's gender conscious organising', *Norma*, 1 (1): 62–81.

Hearn, J. (2006) 'The implications of information and communications technologies for sexualities and sexualised violences: contradictions of sexual citizenship', *Political Geography*, 25: 944–63.

Hearn, J and Pringle K. with members of CROME (2006) *European Perspectives on Men and Masculinities: National and Transnational Approaches*, Hampshire: Palgrave Macmillan.

Heath, S. (1987) 'Male feminism' in *Men in feminism*, (eds) A. Jardine and P. Smith, USA: Routledge, 1–32.

Heelas, P. (1996) 'Introduction: detraditionalization and its rivals' in P. Heelas, S. Lash and P. Morris (eds) *Detraditionalization*, Oxford: Blackwell, 1–14.

Hester, M. (1984) 'Anti-sexist men', *Women's Studies International Forum*, 7 (1): 33–37.

Holter, O.G. (1997) *Gender, Patriarchy and Capitalism: A Social Reform Analysis*, Oslo: University of Oslo.

—— (2003) *Can Men Do It? Men and Gender Equality – The Nordic Experience*, Copenhagen: Nordic Council of Ministers.

Hooks, b. (1998) 'Men as comrades in struggle' in D. Ewing and P. Schacht *Men and Feminism: Reconstructing Gender Relationships* (eds) New York: New York University Press, 119–45.

Hoch, P. (1979) *White Hero, Black Beast: Racism, Sexism and the Mask of Masculinity*, UK: Pluto Press.

Irvine, L. and Klocke, B. (2001) 'Redefining men: alternative masculinities in a twelve-step program', *Men and Masculinities*, 4 (1): 27–48.

Jardine, A. and Smith, P. (eds) (1987) *Men in Feminism*, New York: Routledge.

James, J. (1998) 'Anti-racist (pro)feminisms and coalition politics: "no justice, no peace"' in T. Digby (ed.) *Men Doing Feminism*, USA: Routledge, 237–54.

Jefferson, T. (2002) 'Subordinating hegemonic masculinities' *Theoretical Criminology*, 6 (1) 63–88.

Kaufman, M. (ed.) (1987) *Beyond Patriarchy: Essays by Men on Pleasure, Power and Change*, Toronto: Oxford University Press.

Kaufman, C. A. (1990) 'The anti-politics of identity', *Socialist Review*, 20, 67–80.

Kaufman, M. (1993) *Cracking the Armour: Power, Pain and the Lives of Men* Viking: Toronto.

——and Kimmel, K. (1994) 'Weekend warriors: the new men's movement', in H. Brod and M. Kaufman (eds) *Theorizing Masculinities*, USA: Sage, 259–87.

Kaye, M. and Tolmie, J. (1998) 'Discoursing dads: the rhetorical devises of father's rights groups', *Melbourne University Law Review* 12: 162–94.

——(1987) 'The contemporary crisis of masculinity in historical perspective', in H. Brod (ed.) *The Making of Masculinity: The New Men's Studies*, London: Allen and Unwin.

——and Messer M. (eds) (1989) *Men's Lives*, London: Macmillan.

Kimmel, M. and Mosmiller (1992) *Against the Tide: Profeminist Men in the US 1776–1990: A Documentary History*, Boston, MA: Beacon Press.

——(1994) 'Masculinity as homophobia', in H. Brod and M. Kaufman (eds) *Theorising Masculinities*, Thousand Oaks, CA: Sage, 119–37.

——(ed.) (1995) *The Politics of Manhood: Profeminist Men Respond to the Mythopoetic Men's Movement*, Philadelphia, PA: Temple University Press.

——and Kaufman, M. (1995) 'Weekend warriors: the new men's movement', in M. Kimmel (ed.) *The Politics of Manhood: Profeminist Men Respond to the Mythopoetic Men's Movement*, USA: Temple University Press, 15–43.

——(1996) *Manhood in America: A Cultural History*, USA: Free Press.

——(1998) 'Who's afraid of men doing feminism?' in T. Digby (ed.) *Men Doing Feminism*, USA: Routledge, 57–69.

Kruks, S. (2001) *Subjectivity and Recognition in Feminist Politics: Retrieving Experience*, Ithaca, NY and London: Connell University Press.

Laclau, E. and Mouffe, C. (1985) *Hegemony and Socialist Strategy*, London: Verso.

Laraña, E., Johnson H. and Gusfield, R. (1994) *New Social Movements: From Ideology to Identity*, Philadelphia, PA: Temple University Press.

Lloyd, G. (1984) *Man of Reason*, London: Methuen.

Lloyd, M., (1993) 'The (f)utility of a feminist Turn to Foucault', *Economy and Society*, 22 (4): 437–60.

——(1996) 'A feminist mapping of Foucauldian politics' in S. Hekman (ed.) *Feminist Interpretations of Michel Foucault*, University Park, PA: Pennsylvania, University Press, 437–59.

——(2005) *Beyond Identity Politics*, Thousand Oaks, CA: Sage.

Lyndon, N. (1992) *No More Sex Wars*, London: Sinclair Stevenson.

Mac An Ghaill, M. (ed.) (1996) *Understanding Masculinities: Social Relations and Cultural Arenas*, UK: Open University Press.

MacInnes, J. (1998) *The End of Masculinity*, UK: Open University Press.

MacKinnon, C. (1987) *Feminism Unmodified: Discourses on Life and Law*, London: Harvard University Press.

——(1989) *Toward a Feminist Theory of the State*, London: Harvard University Press.

MacKinnon (1991) 'From practice to theory or what is a white woman anyway?' *Yale Journal of Law and Feminism*, (4): 13–22.

——(1993) *Only words*, London: Harvard University Press.

Mc Carthy, J. D. and Zald, M. (1973) *The Trend of Social Movements in America: Professionalization and Resource Mobilization*, Morristown, NJ: General Learning Press.

McLaren, M. (2002) *Feminism, Foucault and Embodied Subjectivity*, New York: State University of New York Press.

McMahon, A. (1993) 'Male readings of feminist theory: the pyschologization of sexual politics in masculinity literature', *Theory and Society*, 22 (5): 58–71.

Melucci, A. (1985) '*The symbolic challenge of contemporary social movements*', *Social Research*, 52: 789–816.

—— (1989) *Nomads of the Present*, London: Hutchinson Radius.

—— (1996a) *Challenging Codes*, Cambridge and New York: Cambridge University Press.

—— (1996b) *The Playing Self*, Cambridge: Cambridge University Press.

Metz, C. (1968) *Divorce and Custody for Men*, New York: Doubleday.

Messner, M. (1997) *The Politics of Masculinities: Men in Movements*, Thousand Oaks, CA: Sage.

Messner, M. and Sabo, D. (1994) *Sex, Violence and Power in Sports: Rethinking Masculinity*, Freedom, CA: Crossing Press.

Middleton, P. (1992) *The Inward Gaze: Masculinity and Subjectivity in Modern Culture*, London: Routledge.

Modleski, T. (1991) *Feminism Without Women: Culture and Women in a "Postfeminist" Age*, USA: Routledge.

Moore, S. (1988) 'Getting a bit of the Other', in R. Chapman and J. Rutherford (eds) *Male Order: Unwrapping Men, Unwrapping Masculinity*, UK: Lawrence and Wishart, 165–92.

Morgan, D. (1990) *Discovering Men, Sociology and Masculinities*, UK: Routledge.

Morris, M. (1987) 'In any event', in A. Jardine and P. Smith (eds) (1987) *Men in Feminism*, New York: Routledge, 182–88.

Mort, F. (1988) 'Boys own? masculinity, style and popular culture', in R. Chapman and J. Rutherford (eds) *Male Order: Unwrapping Men, Unwrapping Masculinity*, UK: Lawrence and Wishart, 197–224.

Murray, C. (1995) *The Emerging British Underclass*, London: The Institute of Economic Affairs.

National Coalition of Free Men, (2007a) 'Philosophy'. Online. Available at http://www.ncfm.org/phil:htm (accessed 6 June 2007).

National Congress of Women (1992) *Superwoman Keeps on Going: Understanding the Female Web*, UK: National Congress of Women.

National Organisation for Men Against Sexism, (2007) 'Statement of Principles'. Online. Available http://www.nomas.org/statement_ofprinciples.htm (accessed 14 March 2006).

Nedelmann, B. (1984) 'New political movements and changes in processes of intermediation', *Social Science Information* 23 (6).

Nicholson, L. (1992) *Feminism/Postmodernism*, London: Routledge.

O'Brien, M. (1983) *The Politics of Reproduction*, London: Routledge.

Parish, G. (1992) '*Male supremacy and the men's profeminist movement*', *Oh! Brother.* Online. Available http://www.nostatusquo.com/ACLU/OHBROTHER/retrogeov1.html (accessed 19 March 2007).

Parker, A. (1996) 'Sporting masculinities: gender relations and the body', in M. Mac An Ghaill (ed.) *Understanding Masculinities: Social Relations and Cultural Arenas*, UK: Open University Press, 127–38.

Pateman, C. (1988) *The Sexual Contract*, Standford, CA: Standford University Press.

Pease, B. (2000) *Recreating Men: Postmodern Masculinity Politics*, London: Sage.

Petersen, A. (2003) 'Research on men and masculinities: some implications of recent theory for future work', in *Men and Masculinities*, 6 (1): 54–69.

Pfeil, F. (1995) *White Guys: Studies in Postmodern Domination and Difference*, UK: Verso.

Pleck, J. (1981) *The Myth of Masculinity*, Cambridge, MA: MIT Press.

Plummer, K. (1994) *Telling Sexual Stories*, London: Routledge.

Rapping, E. (1996) *The Culture of Recovery: Making Sense of Sense of the Self-help Movement in Women's Lives*, Boston, MA: Beacon.

Rendall, J. (1985) *The Origins of Modern Feminism: Women in Britain, France and the United States, 1780–1860*, London: Macmillan.

Rich, A. (1976) *Of woman born*, New York: Norton.

Richardson, D. and Robinson, U. (1994) 'Theorising women's studies: the politics of naming', *European Journal of Women's Studies*, 1(1): 11–22, 1994.

Richardson, D. and Robinson, V. (1996) 'Repackaging Women and Feminism: Taking the Heat Off Patriarchy' in *Radically Speaking: Feminism Reclaimed*, D. Bell and R. Klein (eds) 169–78. Australia: Zed Books.

Rowan, J. (1987) *The Horned God*, New York: Routledge.

——(2006) 'Achilles Heel and the anti-sexist men's movement', *Psychotherapy and Politics*, 3 (1): 58–71.

Rowbotham (1983) *Dreams and Dilemmas*, London: Virago.

——, 'The trouble with patriarchy', *New Statesman*, 21/12/1979.

Roper, M. and Tosh, J. (eds) (1991) *Manful Assertions: Masculinities in Britain Since 1800*, UK: Routledge.

Ruddick, S. (1990) *Maternal Thinking: Towards a New Politics of Peace*, London: The Women's Press.

Samuel, A.(1997) 'Gender a certain confusion.' Online. Available http://www.achillesheel.freeuk.om/article18.09htm (accessed 3 May 2006).

Schein, L. (1977) 'Dangers with men's conscious raising groups', in J. Snodgrass, *For Men Against Sexism*, New York: Times Change Press.

Schwalbe, M. (1995) *Unlocking the Iron cage: A Critical Appreciation of the Mythopoetic Men's Movement*, New York: Oxford University Press.

Scott, A. (1990) *Ideology and New Social Movements*, London: Unwin Hyman.

Scott, J. (1992) 'Experience' in J. Butler and J. Scott (ed) *Feminists Theorize the Political*, New York: Routledge, 23–40.

Seidler, V. (1989) *Rediscovering Masculinity: Reason, Language and Sexuality*, London: Routledge.

——(1991a) *Recreating Sexual Politics: Men, Feminism and Politics*, London: Routledge.

——(1991b) (ed.) *The Achilles' Heel Reader: Men, Sexual Politics and Socialism*, London: Routledge.

——(1994) *Unreasonable Men: Masculinity and Social Theory*, London: Routledge.

——(1997) *Man Enough: Embodying Masculinities*, UK: Wiltshire.

——(2006) *Young Men and Masculinities: Global Cultures and Intimate Lives*, London and New York: Zed.

Segal, L. (1990) *Slow Motion: Changing Masculinities, Changing Men*, UK: Virago.

——(1999) *Why Feminism?* Cambridge: Polity.

Spark, R. (1994) 'Gift wrapping the men's movement: Canada's White Ribbon Foundation campaign.' Online. Available http://www.members.-shaw.ca/sparkspeaks/wribbon2.html (accessed 8 June 2005).

Spelman, E. (1990) *Inessential Women: Problems of Exclusion in Feminist Thought*, London: Women's Press.

Staples, R. (1982) *Black Masculinity: The Black Male's Role in American Society*, San Francisco, CA: Black Scholars Press.

Stoltenberg, J. (1990) *Refusing to Be a Man: Essays on Sex and Justice*, revised edition, UK: UCL Press (first published 1980).

—— (2000) *The End of Manhood: A Book for Men of Conscience*, Dutton: New York.

Strauss, S. (1982) *'Traitors to the Masculine Cause': The Men's Campaign for Women's Rights*, Westport, CT: Greenwood.

Tarrow, S. (1994) *Power in Movement: Social Movements, Collective Action and Politics*, Cambridge: Cambridge University Press.

Taylor, V. (1996) *Rock-a-by Baby: Feminism, Identity, and Post-Partum Depression*: New York: Routledge.

Thomas, D. (1993) *Not Guilty: In Defence of the Modern Man*, London: Weidenfield and Nicholson.

Tilley, C. (1978) *From Mobilization to Revolution*, Reading, MA: Addison-Wesley.

Tolson, A. (1977) *The Limits of Masculinity*, London: Tavistock.

Tong, R. (1989) *Feminist Thought: A Comprehensive Introduction*, Boulder, CO: Westview Press.

Touraine, A. (1985) 'An introduction to the study of new social movements', *Social Research*, 52: 749–88.

Tucker, S. (1991) 'Gender fucking, and utopia: an essay in response to John Stoltenberg's', '*Refusing to be a Man*', *Social Text*, 27 (3): 3–34.

United Kingdom's Men's Movement, (1995) *Restoring the Foundations of the Family*, Newport, Gwent: UKMM.

Vance, C. (1989) (ed.) *Pleasure and Danger, Exploring Female Sexuality*, UK: Routledge and Kegan and Paul.

Walby, S. (1990) *Theorising Patriarchy*, Oxford: Blackwell.

Waters, M. (1995) *Globalization*, London: Routledge.

Weeks, J. (1977) *Coming Out: Homosexual Politics in Britain*, London: Quartet.

—— (1986: 2nd edn 2003) *Sexuality*, London: Routledge.

——(1985) *Sexuality and Its Discontents*, London: Routledge.

Wernette, T., Acacia, A. and Scherfenberg, C. (1992) 'Male Pride and Anti-Sexism' in Kimmel and Mosmiller *Against the Tide: Pro-feminist men in the United States 1776–1990*, Boston, MA: Beacon, 424–29.

Wetherell, M. and Edley, N. (1999) 'Negotiating hegemonic masculinity: imaginary positions and psycho–discursive practices, *Feminism and Psychology*, 9 (3): 335–56.

Whitehead, S.M. (1998) 'Hegemonic masculinity revisited', *Gender, Work and Organization*, 6 (1): 58–62.

—— (2002) *Men and Masculinities*, Polity: Cambridge.

Young, I. (1990) *Justice and the Politics of Difference*, Princeton, NJ: Princeton University Press.

Index